The Lette

MACHIAVELLI

The Letters of

MACHIAVELLI

A SELECTION

*Translated and Edited
with an Introduction by*

ALLAN GILBERT

THE UNIVERSITY OF CHICAGO PRESS

ACKNOWLEDGEMENTS

To the Research Council *of Duke University I am in-
debted for assistance over some thirty-five years of Machiavellian studies. The Duke University Press has graciously
allowed the use of the version of the Familiar Letters soon
to be published as part of my comprehensive translation
of Machiavelli in three volumes. I wish also to thank the
University of Pennsylvania for opportunity to write the
Introduction during a pleasant year as visiting professor
of Italian literature.*

The University of Chicago Press, Chicago 60637

Library of Congress Cataloging in Publication Data

Machiavelli, Niccolò, 1469–1527.
  The letters of Machiavelli.

  1. Machiavelli, Niccolò, 1469–1527—Correspondence.
2. Florence (Italy)—Politics and government—1421–1737.
3. Intellectuals—Italy—Correspondence. 4. Statesmen—
Italy—Correspondence. 5. Authors, Italian—16th
century—Correspondence. I. Gilbert, Allan H.,
1888–   II. Title.
DG738.14.M2A4 1988   320.1′092′4 [B]   87–35678
ISBN 0–226–50041–1 (pbk.)

Machiavelli's Letters

[SINCE these letters were not written for publication, literary polish is not to be expected. In their genuineness and the glimpses they provide of the author and his friends, they form the best of autobiographies. Obviously many of the total number Niccolò wrote have not been preserved; many had already perished when his grandson collected what he could. The present collection, though not quite complete, gives most of the letters usually printed. They are all published without omissions.

The numbering is that of Alvisi's edition (Firenze, 1883). Since he includes in his collection letters *to* Machiavelli there are many gaps in the numbering.]

Contents

The Letters of

MACHIAVELLI

❧ I ❧

The Life of Niccolò Machiavelli
1469-1527

Io non giudico né giudicherò mai essere difetto difendere alcuna opinione con le ragioni, sanza volervi usare o l'autoritá o la forza (Discorsi 1.58).

[*I do not judge nor shall I ever judge it a sin to defend any opinion by giving reasons for it, without trying to employ either ascendency or force.*]

FLORENCE. 1469. The city and the time of the early Medici. What better place and time for the birth of a man who would look into men's hearts and speak to the ages to follow? In the Florence of this period, the work of Cosimo, Father of his Country, patron of the revival of learning, had just ended, and soon the more celebrated age of Lorenzo the Magnificent was to begin. However much the qualities of this city and this age have been sentimentalized and made romantic, the reality is still wonderful.[1]

As a young man Niccolò Machiavelli was not in a position, as it seems, to share to the utmost in the advantages his city could offer. His family was of some consequence; one earlier Machiavelli had played such a prominent, if unfortunate, part in the constant political strife of the city that Niccolò could mention him, for honest historical reasons, in his *History of Florence*. Though Ber-

[1] Indeed a corrective to conventional views is the elevation of the other cities of Italy rather than the depression of Florence. No small amount of what she had to offer was to be found in other Italian cities. Rome, Ferrara, these and others could in various ways surpass the city on the Arno.

13

nardo, Niccolò's father, was not a rich man, he had a house on Via Guicciardini, south of the Arno, on the way from the Ponte Vecchio to the Pitti Palace. He owned also a house and land in the country, at Sant'Andrea in Percussina, some six miles to the south, near San Casciano. His holdings were hardly extensive enough to be called an estate, though the house, still standing, hints at resources greater than Bernardo seems to have possessed. In his volume of *Ricordi* we find a man able to live comfortably, though not richly, on his ancestral property, and lacking energy or ability or desire to undertake any of the commercial or financial enterprises that sometimes showered wealth on the merchant princes of Florence and provided their assistants with large incomes. There is no indication that Bernardo Machiavelli could provide any special advantages for his children.

Yet advantages Niccolò did somehow secure; in fact, so far as we can judge, he had as good an education as did the most conspicuous Florentine of his day, Lorenzo the Magnificent, only twenty years his senior. In one respect, however, Lorenzo had better opportunities than Niccolò: wealth enabled him to have training in horsemanship and in the use of weapons, so that he could win prizes in the spectacular jousting which still played a large part in Florentine entertainments. Our only knowledge of Machiavelli as sportsman comes from his statement that he indulges in the "pitiful" avocation of setting snares for small birds—the humblest and least demanding sort of hunting [Letter no. 137]. If any teachers affected him, he has not left us their names. Indeed, once having mastered the elements of Latin, he hardly needed instruction for getting what he wished from the history and poetry of the past. (He probably did not study Greek.) In these early years he laid the foundation of his knowledge of Latin literature, whether from instruction in school or by his own efforts alone. At that time, also, much of his reading in Dante, Petrarch, and other Italian authors may have been done, and command acquired over Italian metres, which he was later to employ in his own works. In his studies he would have been aided by the printed books now supplementing the manuscripts to which his predecessors had been limited, though manuscripts were employed for practical use, and were not yet rarities, as Niccolò could observe in his father's library. Of this we learn from Bernardo's volume of *Ricordi*.

There are several entries on Niccolò's schooling in the *Ricordi*. At the age of seven he was one day entrusted with five soldi, the monthly fee of his teacher, Maestro Matteo, who lived at the foot of Ponte Santa Trinità on the south side of Arno. So we are to imagine young Niccolò winding his way through the streets clutching his coins, as reliable even then as Soderini found him in maturity. He was, at that time, learning the elements of Latin from the *Donatello*, or brief *Donatus*, the Latin grammar book of the time. A few months later his teacher was Ser Battista di Filippo da Poppi, whose school was in the church of San Benedetto dallo Studio in Via dello Studio, a few steps south of the Piazza del Duomo. To reach this school, the boy, starting in Via Guicciardini, would almost at once have crossed the Ponte Vecchio. Then he could have varied his route, choosing to pass, for example, the palace of the Art of Wool or, turning to the right, walk through the Piazza della Signoria in front of the Palazzo Vecchio (then the Palace of the Signoria) and on past Orsanmichele. Thus he went twice a day through the heart of the city, almost to Santa Maria del Fiore, more than half a mile from home. Florence early made her impression on him.

Ser Battista lent Bernardo a Pliny in Italian and received on loan Macrobius' *Somnium Scipionis* and *Saturnalia*, so the two had common interests. Was he chosen for that reason? Still more important for the father's intellectual associations was his acquaintance with the humanist Bartolommeo Scala, first chancellor of Florence for years, who in his *De regibus et judiciis* represents Bernardo as visiting him at his house in the Borgo Pinti and engaging in dialogue with him.

At ten years of age, Niccolò went to a teacher of arithmetic, and at twelve he studied Latin under still another master. Though Bernardo's notes go some years further, nothing more is said on his son's schooling. In a letter of April 1527 [no. 222] Niccolò mentions his studies in letters and music when exhorting his son Guido to pursue those subjects. Presumably he has in mind his own schooling, however much supplemented by his personal efforts.

In Bernardo's library or among the volumes he borrowed up to Niccolò's eighteenth year, when the entries cease, are some books that did excellent service to the author of the *Discourses* and *The History of Florence*. In 1475 Bernardo agreed to prepare for Nicolò Tedesco, "priest and astrologer," a geographical index of Livy; in return he received a printed copy of Livy's *Histories*. Eleven years later he took to the binder what appears to have been another edition of Livy. The young Niccolò, then, had opportunity to become familiar with the historian on whom he founded his *Discourses*. In 1485 Bernardo bought the *Decades* of Blondius, from which Niccolò drew material for his *History of Florence*. He owned also the same author's *Italia Illustrata*. Many of his purchases were law books. There is no indication that he owned any poetry.

Whatever Niccolò's schooling, however assiduous his private reading, a great part of his education came from the city of Florence. So small was the area within her mediaeval walls that her centers could be reached on foot in a few minutes from the house on Via Guicciardini. Life, for men at least, was to a large extent lived in the public square, or loggia. Here resorted Florentines who were not held to their workshops by the nature of their employment. The mass of inhabitants were occupied in the silk business or the manufacture of wool, or in similar occupations. They seldom appeared in public. But the relatively few who had command of their time spent part of it in public places, often transacting business there. Men of similar interests formed the habit of coming to some such place as the Loggia of the Tornaquinci almost every day. There, according to their interests, they discussed commerce, politics, Latin poetry, modern literature, the sermons preached at the Duomo or at Santa Croce, and an eager young man might stand on the outskirts of a circle of important men to hear their opinions. What went on in the wide world interested these Florentines, and they had a long tradition of speaking their minds. Pungent wit often made their remarks worth hearing; a good talker had an audience. Niccolò would often have been part of such groups, to listen and to speak—not too often or at too great length, certainly. Even when the talk at such places descended to mere gossip, he would still have profited as one who by nature loved to draw general concepts from the individual sayings and doings of men, and thus even from folly could draw wisdom. In these continual public gatherings it rapidly became apparent who was interested in various topics and could speak well—or listen well—when they were discussed. Hence, more restricted meetings were easily formed, at which the common interests and the ability of those present had fuller scope. Such assemblies would not always have had an intellectual purpose; they may sometimes have had an opposite purpose, but at least they winnowed out the misfits, and they furnished those present with what they expected. In this informal university Machiavelli, interested more in wisdom and in human nature than in erudition for its own sake, would have learned many lessons.

Niccolò last appears in the *Ricordi* when he was eighteen. After that we know nothing of him until ten years later, in 1497, if that is the date of two letters about family property, one of them in Latin. During these years he probably wrote some of his Carnival Songs and perhaps other poems. Through some sort of activity, employment or achievement, he made his abilities known, probably to various men of position and influence.

In 1498 he was a candidate for the position of Second Chancellor or Secretary. This was the second most important paid position in the government of Florence. In his first attempt at the post he was unsuccessful; then later in the year he was elected, at an annual salary of two hundred sealed florins. That he was elected at the age of twenty-nine to such an important post has led to speculation that he had earlier held some lesser government office, but there is no evidence for this. Clearly he had been in no position that he considered political, for on 10 December 1513 he wrote to Vettori that he had been studying the art of government for fifteen years, evidently counting from the time of his election. Had he earlier held a government post, he would hardly have failed to count its years among those devoted to learning statecraft. So we can only feel sure that during his early manhood he was becoming known as one on whose ability and devotion Florence could rely.

Three types of business came under the view of important Florentine officials. First, there was the internal government of an independent city, whose laws were determined only from within. Second, Florence ruled a Tuscan empire, made up of large rural areas and of other cities, as Pistoia, Prato, Arezzo and, at times, Pisa. These cities enjoyed some local privileges but were under constant Florentine supervision; they were subjects, with no voice in the control of the empire. Third, Florence was one of the independent states of Italy, owing allegiance to no one, and dealing directly with the most powerful monarchs, such as the King of France. So Machiavelli as Secretary had his part in international negotiations as well as in the domestic business of the city. In the summer of 1499, he went on a mission to the formidable Countess of Forlì, by whom he was quietly amused. The next year he was sent to France; to that country he returned three times in the course of his fifteen years in office. He went twice to the papal court. The first six months of 1508 he spent on a mission to the Emperor Maximilian, and was again at his court the next year. For nearly four months, beginning in October 1502, he was with Cesare Borgia. Then there were various missions within the Florentine dominion, especially his service with the army operating against Pisa in 1509. From 1506 to 1512 he was often in rural Tuscany on the business of enrolling and supplying the countrymen trained as soldiers according to his plan. (This army was a sort of provincial militia.) Apart from this service, his recorded absences from the city on business total some three and a half years. When his travels in the Florentine dominion are added, it appears that he spent a quarter or a third of his period of service in the field rather than at his desk in the City Hall.

The government under which Machiavelli spent the actively political part of his life differed in two ways from the usual Florentine organization. First, the Medici family was in exile. After the triumph of Cosimo de' Medici's party in 1434, it had exercised effective control in city affairs until the expulsion of Piero, the great-grandson of Cosimo, in 1494. Its direct power was most evident during the period after the Pazzi conspiracy (1478) in which Giuliano de' Medici was murdered, that is, during the career of Lorenzo the Magnificent, who died in 1492.

Second, about four years after Machiavelli received his secretarial position, Piero Soderini was made Gonfalonier for life. Florence then had a permanent head for her government. Before, even during the Medici control, the loose official organization was similar to that satirized by Dante two centuries earlier, when he addressed the city:

> Athens and Lacedemonia, which made their ancient laws and were so well organized, made but a slight gesture toward good government compared with you, who make such clever provisions that what you spin in October does not last until the middle of November. (*Purgatorio* 6, 139-144).

Astonishing as it seems, the governing officials of Florence were chosen for only two months, so that the city experienced a change of administration six times a year. This—though less often than one might suppose—could cause rapid changes of policy in important matters. However, during more than half of Machiavelli's chancellorship, Florence had continuity in her chief official. At other times he worked under the system of continually shifting authority, though the membership of a board of Eight or Ten in charge of important matters—war, for example—could be kept with slight changes for long periods. It is possible to find some justification for the two-months system, however. During the two months for which the Signoria served, its duties required the entire time of its members, who lived in the City Hall, the building now called the Palazzo Vecchio. To "go home" openly was to resign office. The members were not professional politicians but business men; while they served the city, they neglected their private affairs. More than two months of such complete neglect could not reasonably be required of them. In the course of Machiavelli's service, the direct demands on the Signoria were perhaps reduced; at any rate, when on an early diplomatic mission, he addressed his official letters to the Signoria until 21

November 1500; then he began to address the Ten of Liberty and Peace. To some such group his reports are addressed during the succeeding years wherever he was serving.

Though such missions had been performed by earlier secretaries, influential men in the city evidently felt that this young official had capacity for more than record-keeping and letter-writing in a bureau. He was able to handle matters of importance. Moreover, the Secretary, being a full-time employee, had no business that he was neglecting; he could be kept in the field as long as was necessary. His situation may have been quite what the cautious Florentine administrators wished. They had a competent, hard-working, trustworthy man looking after their affairs, a man whom even Cesare Borgia or the King of France must take seriously, yet not of such high position in the city that any unfortunate action on his part was likely to embarrass them. They could even indulge in procrastination (one of the vices Machiavelli attributed to their governing officials—*Discourses* 2.15) by withholding ambassador's rank from their representative. Such an honor could go only to a man whose family had more rank and influence than did Machiavelli's. The Secretary might complain that the Ten did not allow him expense money enough; he might—under a thin disguise not intended to deceive any shrewd member of the board—advise his superiors on the wisest policy. Yet he could get on with foreigners of rank and authority, and he sent back to Florence frequent and informative reports.

Important among these diplomatic journeys were those to the Lady of Forlì (Caterina Sforza), to Cesare Borgia at the time when he out-tricked and executed his treacherous mercenary captains, to the Court of France (where Niccolò was sent three times), to the Pope, Julius II, at Rome, and to the Emperor Maximilian I. For four months

21

he was Florentine agent at Cesare Borgia's court at Imola and at other places; some six months were required for the mission to Emperor Maximilian. Clearly, Piero Soderini felt that the Secretary had great ability in the practical management of affairs.

Reflecting upon his experience abroad, Niccolò developed it into a body of practical advice for an ambassador, as appears in a letter to Raffaelo Girolami, the Florentine ambassador to Spain. In part Machiavelli reveals what he himself actually did, in part what he would have done if holding higher rank and provided with more money. He explains that he speaks out of his experience, "not in presumption but in affection."

An ambassador needs such a reputation that he can get the ear of the monarch with whom he deals; accomplishing this, he makes hard things easy. To this end he must by his conduct show that he is able, liberal and, above all, trustworthy, not tricky. There are men who though prudent yet, being two-faced, have so alarmed a prince that they have not been able to deal with him. Alessandro Neri gained great honor in France because he was believed honest and straightforward; others have been disgraced because believed the reverse of that. While on his mission to Cesare Borgia, Niccolò wrote that he was trying in every way to get Cesare to trust him and to talk intimately with him.

An ambassador must gather information on matters that the ruler and his advisers are considering. Hence he must cultivate men likely to know about official discussions who will repeat what they learn. Very grave men have made use of banquets and entertainments in their houses to gain easy opportunity to talk with such persons. Since men do not give out information without some return, the ambassador must get officials at home to send him information of every sort, even seemingly trivial, about events discussed widely in the country he is visiting. From the men to whom he listens the ambassador will get a mass of truth and falsehood. From this he must select what is valuable, discarding the rest; then he will form his conclusions. These the envoy will be careful not to put abruptly before authorities at home, as though he were trying to dictate policy. He should hide behind some flimsy barricade such as declaring that "the prudent men he meets believe the outcome will be of a certain sort," and so on. Machiavelli himself used this method on his mission to Cesare Borgia, giving in detail the arguments of a "friend" to show that Florence would profit if she gave up attempting to deal with Cesare with vague general talk and secured his favor and assistance through a specific alliance. Machiavelli never could carry out his suggestion about invitations that would bring information, since he was limited by his slender funds; a wealthy ambassador would not restrict himself to the public funds provided, but would dip into his own purse.

The wise ambassador will inform himself about the country into which he is sent. For example: Does the Emperor prefer to live in Spain or in Flanders? Is he popular? Does France have friends in Spain? What does the Emperor intend to do in Italy? The foreign agent is to send such information to his government at home. Nor should he be content with sending it once, but is to repeat his information every two or three months, "dressing it up anew with such skill, and adding new events, that the repetition may seem to result from prudence and necessity and not from foolish presumption." Machiavelli practised this method also. Thus his *Picture of French Affairs*, commonly considered one of his historical works, is evidently intended for the practical purposes of his ambassadorial friend. So Machiavelli's writings on France, on Germany, and on Lucca are to be taken as notes or drafts for such a purpose, perhaps such as skill and prudence found no opportunity to use. To one so assiduously directing himself to learn what might be of value to Florence, experience in observing men and affairs in other places was of the highest value.

Moreover, the careful reports he wrote are, to some extent, preliminary drafts for his famous works. They show him serving an apprenticeship in writing simply, informatively and interestingly enough to catch, he hoped, the eyes of Florentine rulers. Niccolò Valori wrote of the despatches he sent from Cesare Borgia's court in 1502, that they could not be more highly approved. Piero Soderini, the Gonfalonier for life, judged that the Secretary was doing so well that he should not be relieved of the duties which, sickened by insufficient money and lack of authority to settle anything with Cesare, he wished to abandon.

These golden opinions from the Gonfalonier and other influential Florentines led to Machiavelli's most spectacular service in which he broke into the field normally reserved for Florentines of richer and more influential families. He was given responsibility and authority in the conduct of the campaign against Pisa, Florence's most unwilling subject, frequently in revolt. He was actually in the field with Florentine troops in the spring of 1509 and personally directed operations. Thus he gained practical experience in some of those military matters that he had observed when on his legations to Borgia and to the Emperor. Nevertheless his duties did not require the active command of troops, but rather their maintenance and supply. Yet he did make and see to the execution of strategic decisions, especially when he advised on the assuming of military positions for cutting off supplies from Pisa. Something of the sort had earlier been done by Florentine civilian commissioners like Antonio Pucci and Bernardo del

Nero at the siege of Pietrasanta in 1484, as Niccolò was to say in his *History of Florence*, 8.31. His difficulties were especially great in that he was not a commissioner. Such officials were already on the ground, so that Machiavelli, though only a chancellor, was obliged to take their authority out of their hands and push through the measures they should have attempted. His conduct was approved by the government at Florence, though Soderini did suggest that the active campaigner should give more show of consideration for the legally appointed commissioner. Was Niccolò negligent in this respect in his stress of business? The whole affair, with the successful outcome of the campaign, indicates that when the Secretary had the opportunity to apply the methods of the successful ruler and general as he presents them in his writings, he had the capacity to do so. Fortune used the poverty and low rank of his family to keep him from other positions in which his executive talent could be displayed.

In the course of the operations against Pisa, he was the proponent of an engineering operation that failed, namely an effort to divert the Arno from her course through Pisa, thus depriving the city of a natural moat. How thoroughly he believed in the competence of the North Italian engineers employed, we cannot now tell. If he had considered the diversion a good example of siege tactics, might he not have mentioned it in his *Art of War*? But at the time when that work was published, he was not in a position to emphasize that he had held a responsible post under Soderini. At least the Pisan campaign gave him a close view of military operations as carried on in part by mercenary troops, and in part by Tuscan militia.

A few years later he spoke impartially of the resistance of Pisa almost as though he approved it (*Prince* 5). Certainly his power to see and speak objectively and fairly was not affected by his military activities. Yet he carried on his duties against Pisa as actively and intelligently as he did others assigned to him. If he had an opportunity to give his opinion on the Pisan venture, he probably spoke against it, yet moderately and without the reformer's feeling of absolute right (*Discourses* 3. 35). When policy-makers in Florence decreed violence against Pisa and assigned Machiavelli an important part in it, he had no scruples against accepting. If a policy is to be carried through, (runs the tacit argument), is Niccolò the secretary, in this world of uncertainties and strange results, to refuse to play his part? If he can do better than others, should he not handle as well as possible even a bad policy that is sure to be carried out with or without him? If Florence is determined to take Pisa by force, will it not be better that she shall succeed quickly? At least Machiavelli could do something to make the terms of surrender mild and the occupation of the city without cruelty.

There was another policy on which Machiavelli spent years and in which he believed even after its apparent failure. Identified with him is the attempt to provide Florence with weapons and an army of her own, not those of some doubtfully loyal or even completely disloyal mercenary captain, fighting for his own advantage. If Florence was to expand her empire, or even to defend herself against her many foes, the Secretary believed that she could not rely on her wealth alone; she must have armies led by her own citizens, made up of her inhabitants. From this position the obvious policy to be adopted is military training within the walls of Florence, such as Livy described as normal in Rome.

The reality that resulted from Machiavelli's six years of labor was far inferior to Roman achievements. In the timid scheme inaugurated by Florence in 1506 not a single dweller within the city walls took up arms, only men living in the country districts of Tuscany. This, however useful, was merely a start toward an effective program. Doubtless some details were the originator's own, reflections of which are to be found in the *Discourses* or *The Art of War.* Considering the passages on arms in those works, we may suppose that he favored the notion of arming at least ten of every hundred infantrymen with firearms, while seventy carried the pikes of the Swiss, "the teachers of modern wars." Similarly, he may well have suggested the clause found in the official papers on the militia that three or four or more bands should be arquebusiers, trained to handle this clumsy ancestor of the rifle. As he had Fabrizio Colonna say in *The Art of War*, this new weapon is "necessary" (Bk 2); and he gives it to one-sixth, not one-tenth, of his infantry, perhaps because the author is keeping up with the progress of military practice. But as a secretary he would always present what he could get approved by the authorities, not what he believed advisable. The details were apparently in his hands: enrollment of men, supply of weapons, appointment of minor officers, disbursement of money. In the years from 1506 to 1512 much of his time was spent in the Florentine dominion on militia business.

At present, when Machiavelli is viewed chiefly as a writer, the years of diplomacy and military activity up to 1512 seem devoted only to his preparation for authorship. Not that he wrote only official letters during this period. In 1504 he produced his *First Decennale,* or *Poem of Ten Years*, surveying Florentine history from the expulsion of the Medici in 1494. These verses show that he had already practised the writing of *terza rima* enough to gain control of that metrical form, and that although an active public servant he did not forget Dante and Petrarch. Apparently, too, he kept up his reading in Latin literature and history. He read Greek literature in translation; for example when, as we know, he read Xenophon's *Life of Cyrus,* he might have used either the Latin of Poggio Bracciolini or the Italian of Poggio's son, who was executed for his part in the Pazzi Conspiracy. Machiavelli's grandson assigns to the year 1504 a play called *The Masks,* in imitation of Aristophanes, so satirical of various Florentines that he was unwilling to copy fragments he found among his grandfather's papers. If *The Masks* is so early, may not some of Niccolò's other dramatic writings, such as *Clizia,* his imitation of Plautus' *Casina,* be earlier than is sometimes supposed? However that may be, throughout his life Niccolò was a man of letters as well as a politician.

With his constant interest in mankind at every level, with his genius as a story-teller (he was praised by Bandello for this, *Novelle* I. 46), and his pleasant disposition, Machiavelli was socially in demand, and probably spent much time in the various assemblies that made Florentine life pleasant. From one such assembly a trifle among his verses seems to have resulted, an epigram running as follows:

> La notte che morì Pier Soderini,
> L'anima andò de l'inferno a la bocca;
> Gridò Pluton: "Ch'inferno? Anima sciocca,
> Va su nel limbo fra gli altri bambini."

On the night when Piero Soderini died, his soul went to the mouth of Hell. Pluto yelled: "Why are you in Hell? Silly soul, go up into Limbo with the other babies."

Such verses were, in the Renaissance, often composed for diversion. At a banquet (we may suppose), where the Gonfalonier and the witty Secretary were both guests, the company turned to comic epitaphs. As the most prominent man present, Soderini would be a natural center of interest. The best effort would be expected from the Secretary, who may have come prepared; or are we to think that he worked on the inspiration of the moment?

28

However that may be, Niccolò had in mind one or two passages from Dante. Virgil addresses Nimrod in Hell as "silly soul," as Pluto does Soderini, and Machiavelli knew from Dante, as well as from theologians, of unbaptised infants in Limbo. Therefore he had the material ready for delighting Soderini and the whole assembly.

In 1512 the course of Machiavelli's life abruptly changed, Tuscany was invaded by a Spanish army supporting the exiled Medici. Such influence as Machiavelli had with the government was not enough to secure adequate military preparation. On such as had been made was the impress of his mind, for among the defenders of the city of Prato, attacked by the Spanish, were some of the countrymen on whose military training the Secretary had labored for six years. Whether because poorly led, because disaffected, or because frightened by the Spanish soldiers, war-hardened veterans who had made good their retreat from the lost battle of Ravenna, the Tuscan militia, both pikemen and musketeers, made slight resistance. We have no reason to believe that their organizer was astonished or seriously disappointed by their failure; he had read too much and seen too much to count on certainties in war; he also had some respect for the Spanish mercenaries. Moreover, his theory required that Prato be defended by the men of Prato, and Florence by Florentine citizens. After a display of weakness and arrogance, Florence opened her gates to the enemy, Soderini left the city, and the Medici were once more rulers.

Less prominent than we are now likely to assume—being then only secretary and not famous author—Machiavelli was yet a conspicuous member of the overthrown government. He nevertheless remained in Florence. Is it possible that he had some hope that he would not be disturbed, even that the Medici would retain him in office? He accepted the failure of the government he favored. Against the Medici there was no use in struggling. Their rule was what Florence wanted; it must be borne. For many years the city had found the control of the now-restored family acceptable; could it more completely fail to defend Tuscany than had Soderini's regime? So the Secretary accepted the inevitable. If the Medici government was to be restored in blood, the blame would in no way be his. For a short time it seemed that for him individually his policy of nonresistance would succeed. Not until about seven weeks after the return of the Medici was he deprived of his secretaryship. Then he was forbidden, under bond, to leave the Florentine dominion for a year, and ordered not to enter the City Hall for the same period. In February 1513 he was suspected of complicity in a foolishly hopeless conspiracy against the Medici. The *Discourses on Livy* were still unwritten; yet even if the Mediceans could have read the chapter (3.6) in which he sets forth the folly of conspiracy, they probably could hardly have believed that he had the firmness to put his theory into practice. Thrown into prison, he was tortured on the rack (perhaps rather mildly), in accord with the judicial habits of the time. For this torture no legal records have been presented by biographers. The evidence consists of his grandson's statement, an oblique reference in Letter no. 120, and a tailed sonnet addressed to Giuliano de'Medici (son of Lorenzo the Magnificent) then representing the family in the city. A poem, especially a comic poem, is not to be relied on for accuracy. Yet torture of a prisoner suspected of conspiracy against a new government is so likely that we should accept it, with admiration for the courage and temperance that enabled the sufferer to see it as comic. With many others, he was released from prison to celebrate the election to the papal throne of Giovanni de'Medici, in March 1513, as Pope Leo X.

Apparently Machiavelli and his family did not leave their

house in Via Guicciardini for the villa at Sant'Andrea in Percussina until after his release from prison. At least he says in a letter of 10 December 1513 that since his last troubles (evidently his imprisonment) he has not spent twenty days in Florence. For this abandonment of the city the reason seemingly was financial. The cheapest food was that produced on his own land. Perhaps the house in Florence could be rented. Yet only three of his letters are dated from Sant'Andrea; all the rest are written as from Florence. To be sure, the village is but six miles from Florence, so near, indeed, that Brunelleschi's dome, the "hupola" of people at Sant'Andrea, is part of the landscape. Possibly Machiavelli still possessed a horse or a mule that he could ride to Florence; or in that day men were still able to walk.

Though Niccolò was probably less successful than his father in managing his landed property, his decision on a procedure which enabled him to exist on his small income is not strange to any reader who has observed the financial integrity characterizing his father's *Book of Records*. Sant'Andrea furnished proof that Niccolò had not taken for himself any part of the considerable sums of public money that passed through his hands, and about which the Florentine authorities had questioned him after his dismissal from office. In his eyes, public office was a public trust, not a source of personal financial gain. To Vettori he wrote:

Of my honesty there should be no doubt, because having always preserved my honesty, I shall hardly now learn how to break it; and he who has been honest and good for forty-three years, as I have, cannot change his nature; and of my honesty and goodness I have as a witness my poverty" (No. 137).

Had Machiavelli been corruptible, he would not have needed to move to Sant'Andrea.

Such an assertion of honesty on the part of an official

whose influence with a government could secure financial and other benefits may meet with half-incredulous acceptance in our day or any day. Much misunderstood has been the dismissed Secretary's attempt to regain a governmental position, and when that failed to get employment with the Medicean régime controlling Florence. Moralists have adopted a simplified view of conditions, and have said: "The Medici were tyrants; Machiavelli believed in liberty. *Ergo* he should have been a bitter enemy of the tyrants, rejecting with indignation any thought of taking pay from them." But the matter can be more liberally considered. What blame at present would be laid upon a career diplomat who retained his position when a Republican régime in Washington gave place to a Democratic one? Machiavelli's situation was similar. Assuredly he preferred control more general than that by a single family; this he made clear a few years later when, along with others, he received a Medici request to suggest the best sort of government for Florence. Yet Soderini's own administration failed because, as Niccolò indicates in his *Discourses* 3.9, its leader was unwilling to engage in severe and even violent measures against Medici supporters. Those measures would have required tyrannical action. After having done what was required, Soderini might not have resumed his constitutional position, whether because of adverse conditions or because he became intoxicated with power. When he failed, the alternative was the Medici party, which had sufficient support to continue in control for fifteen years, almost as long as its predecessor. The violence of the Medici restoration need not be much emphasized; such was Florentine custom. Since under any rule Florence was still Machiavelli's native city and still required public officials, he was willing to serve the only government that, as his good sense and clear view of the world enabled him to realize, could then sustain itself there.

Knowing mankind as he did, Machiavelli did not think it strange that he lost his position, or even that he was suspected of knowing about the conspiracy against the Medici. It was as natural for the Mediceans to suspect him as it was for those concerned in the abortive plot to think of Machiavelli as one who—a friend to Soderini—would strive for his restoration. Party feeling was expected to surpass patriotism. Niccolò did not hope for his old position; indeed he mentions employment at Rome or by the Pope, where he could prove himself in a position less suspect than any at Florence (Letter no. 122). If partisanship was then violent, men also passed easily from one party to another; many citizens of Florence had been in some way implicated in the non-Medicean government. So Machiavelli could hope that influence, supported by knowledge of his ability, would bring him something suitable. Slowly, very slowly in the eyes of a man deprived of most of the income and activity he had enjoyed for fourteen years, time justified his stand. Before many years he did receive employment from the Medici, not only the commission to write a history of Florence, but even, almost at the end of his life, the appointment as executive secretary of the commission in charge of the city fortifications. About the salary he may have received for this work, nothing is known.

Machiavelli attempted to find suitable occupation in two ways. One was to ask the influence of friends, especially Francesco Vettori, to whom many of his letters in 1512 and afterward are written. But characteristically he also did what he could for himself; that is, he composed *The Prince,* which he planned to present to Giuliano de' Medici as proof and reminder of his competence. In such action he was following in the steps of humanists who obtained important political employment, such men as Petrarch, Pontanus and Poggio Bracciolini; his coeval Baldassare Castiglione was at the same time composing *The Courtier,* the fourth book of which is an analogue to a section of *The Prince*. A few years later Agostino Nifo, by a Latin paraphrase of the unpublished *Prince*, with some additions, hoped to make himself secure in the favor of the Emperor Charles V. So Niccolò's plan was not unreasonable.

To the years after Machiavelli lost his office the greater part of his writing is evidently to be assigned, though usually we have only dates of completion or publication, not those of composition. He was working on *The Prince* in December 1513, as we learn in a letter of the time (No. 137). Whether the little book then assumed its present form is less certain. On the *Discourses* he worked for some years, probably beginning in 1512. Indeed what we have is not entirely ready for publication, and more was planned. *The Art of War* was printed in 1520. Its ideas would have been at the author's command by 1512. *The Life of Castruccio Castracani* is dated in 1520 by Machiavelli's long visit to Lucca on business that left him much leisure. Presumably he would not have undertaken *The History of Florence* had he not obtained from the Cardinal Giulio de'Medici, later Pope Clement VII, a commission to write it in 1521.

On the dates of the plays there is still discussion. The natural order puts first the translation of the *Andria* of Terence, racy and independent, but still a translation. *Clizia*, as an adaptation depending for its plot on the *Casina* of Plautus, would easily come next, to be followed by the original and free *Mandragola*. But such an order is perhaps too persuasive to represent the facts. In *Clizia* there is a reference to some of the characters of *Mandragola*, yet inaccurately, for it would give the friar a major rather than a minor part. Would Machiavelli have referred incorrectly to his own play, or is there some other complexity, such as further revision, or circulation of the story by word of mouth when the play was unknown? The year

1518 has been selected on the ground that a comic character asks: "Do you think the Turk will cross over into Italy this year?" (3.3), and it was in 1518 that fears of invasion were especially strong because of the great military exploits of Selim the Sultan of Turkey. But talk of such an invasion was common after the occupation of Otranto in 1480 by the Turks. In an official letter of 22 April 1499 (Alvisi, no. 4) Machiavelli reports to Piero Francesco Tosinghi, commissioner for military operations against Pisa, on news from Venice, where such fear has been raised by a Turkish fleet that Venice is making preparations to defend her cities in Apulia. On 5 June he adds: "Every day further news about the Turk comes out; some think he is going to Sicily; and it is true that he has made such effort by land and sea that everybody is alert" (Alvisi, no. 5). The Turks continue to be mentioned in letters to Machiavelli, first at Forlì and then in Florence (Alvisi, nos. 7, 8, 9, 10). As late as 16 July 1501, Agostino Vespucci writes from Rome that the Pope "seems to have been frightened by the rumor about the Turks, which still makes a big noise here" (Alvisi, no. 17). On 18 May 1521 Machiavelli refers to this fear of Turkish invasion as one of several stories told by people sitting on benches, evidently such an assemblage as that described near the end of letter 144, where Brancaccio sits telling stories to a crowd. To the stupid comic speaker in *Mandragola* an absurdity of common gossip is more suitable than is a neat historical reference. Since 1520 is the earliest date at which we hear of the comedy, earlier composition would require the author to keep the play by him for some years. For *Clizia* the earliest date of mention is 1524. For *Belfagor*, his short story, we have no date, but Machiavelli would have been capable of any of these works at any time in the last quarter-century of his life. As we have seen, his lost Aristophanic play, *The Masks*, is assigned to 1504.

Being a lover of the city, Niccolò would have been living

in his house on Via Guicciardini rather than in the country as soon after his loss of office as his finances permitted. Since he writes from Sant'Andrea on 4 December 1514, he probably was living there at the time; yet later in the winter his letters are from Florence. In October 1516 he made a journey to Livorno unexplained by his biographers. A letter from that city furnishes ground for an inference that he was carrying on public business; he seems to have remained five days. Not until 8 June 1517 is there another letter—discouraged in tone—from Sant'Andrea, which says: "I am brought to living in the country by the difficulties I have had and now have." Does this indicate that he had for a time been living in the city and is now again in the country? Did some further difficulty arise after his journey to Livorno, or is he speaking only of his continuous poverty? At any rate he did not lose touch with men in the city, for on 3 March 1518 he went to Genoa on business for some Florentine merchants. Since a letter from them dated 8 April deals with the business as incomplete, perhaps he remained in Genoa for several months.

By 1519 Cardinal Giulio de'Medici, the future Pope Clement VII, regarded Machiavelli with enough favor to ask his opinion on the best form of government for Florence. In response Machiavelli wrote his *Discourse on Remodeling the Government of Florence,* advising republican forms, though reserving power to the Medici during their lives. Though this effort hardly went unrewarded, no regular employment resulted. About this time the ex-Secretary may have been occupied with his *Art of War*; at least it was printed in 1521. After the *Discourse* on Florentine government, in 1520 came a mercantile mission to Lucca, with official backing, concerned partly with debts to Florentines, partly with some business of the Mint, and partly with the affairs of some students who had gone to Lucca from the University of Pisa. So now one of Niccolò's friends could write to him as "Secretary in Lucca." This was a shadow of his old position. Having time on his hands, for he spent some three months in Lucca, he characteristically studied the Lucchese system of public administration, in order to carry on his dealings better. He also interested himself in the fourteenth-century Lucchese hero, Castruccio Castracani. The result was the *Life of Castruccio,* presented to two friends in Florence, Zanobi Buondelmonti and Luigi Alamanni. These two are also part of the group represented as listening to the dialogues of *The Art of War.*

With these and others of intellectual importance Machiavelli met in the Rucellai Gardens in Florence. Luigi Alamanni, for example, was a poet whose works are still not unknown. His epic *Girone il-Cortese* won good words from Tasso at the end of the century. The sort of conversation that went on in the Gardens appears, with the embellishments of fiction, in Machiavelli's *Art of War.* To those who met there Machiavelli is said to have read parts of his *Discourses.* For a man of Machiavelli's social gifts and eagerness to learn by hearing as well as by reading, such meetings must have been an unceasing delight.

In November 1520, not long after his return from Lucca, Niccolò received from what we should now call the University of Florence, headed by Cardinal Giulio de'Medici, a commission to write a history of Florence, at an annual salary of one hundred sealed florins. This was also a sort of retainer for other services, so that in May 1521 he went to Carpi to endeavor to secure separate administration for the Franciscans in Florentine territory. In this mission, though backed not only by Cardinal Giulio but even by Pope Leo X himself, he was unsuccessful. Its chief products were the amusing letters written from Carpi to Francesco Guicciardini, Pope Leo's chief official in Lombardy (Nos. 179, 182, 183).

Machiavelli's next public appearance was in 1525, after

the army of the Emperor Charles V defeated and captured King Francis I at Pavia. To present his *History of Florence* to Pope Clement VII he went to Rome. The work had now been brought as far as the death of Lorenzo de'Medici. It was so acceptable that the author received a subsidy for its continuation. More than that, he talked with the Pope on Italian affairs, especially on the defense of Florence against the Imperial army likely to move south. In these conversations he would have appeared as the author of *The Art of War* and as the administrator of the forces drilled in Tuscany before 1512. As a result, he was sent to Francesco Guicciardini, the Pope's representative in the Romagna, with the suggestion for raising troops there. The papal brief he took was so well composed that we may guess it the composition of Niccolò himself. It emphasizes the labor and attention required for executing the plan, and the necessity for popular approval. Guicciardini, as familiar with conditions, can judge. When he reported that the Pope had no friends in the Romagna, Machiavelli, with his belief that a successful prince must be loved by his people, knew that no papal army could be raised in that province.

On his next mission, also in 1525, he went to Venice in the matter of injury done by a Venetian to Florentine merchants and citizens in Lesina. The agent had a letter from the consuls of the Art of Wool in Florence, a letter from the Signoria, and a papal brief. During this absence his name was put among those of citizens eligible for office. We can hardly avoid inferring that the underlying cause was his favor with the Pope, who may have taken this method of rewarding his agent and giving him some greater weight as a negotiator. It may indicate the wiping out of any last suspicion that Niccolò might act as an anti-Medicean.

In May 1526 he again became a regular worker in the Florentine administration. As the imperial army moved south, after its victory at Pavia, Florence was in danger. It had become evident, since—for example—the siege of Padua by the Emperor Maximilian I in 1509, that mediaeval walls were no longer adequate against the "fury of artillery" (*Art of War*, bk 7). Who in Florence better knew this than the author of *The Art of War*, with its section on sieges? His activity both before and after his official appointment appears in his letters to Francesco Guicciardini (Nos. 206, 207, 209, 210). On April 5 he examined the whole circuit of the city wall in the company of the experienced Spanish soldier Count Pietro Navarra. Thereupon he wrote a report of his visit, to be found among his works, showing that fortification, especially the subject of *baluardi* or bastions, had as a result of his instruction by the Count become clearer to him than it had been when he was writing *The Art of War*.

A plan was made for the inspection of Pope Clement VII, without whose approval nothing could be done. Two weeks later Machiavelli complained about delays, for Clement, if he ever saw *The Prince* (chap. 25) did not learn from it the necessity for making dikes betimes against the barbarian deluge. As the chapter indicates, Machiavelli as an administrator could brook no dawdling when an extra day's work might save the city. On the next day the Board of Overseers of the Walls was at last officially constituted, and Machiavelli promptly chosen secretary, that is, executive officer.

Now he could feel completely reinstated in work for which his talents and his studies fitted him. Moreover, he was contributing in the most direct fashion to the defense of his beloved Florence. As when in charge of the militia, he once more rode about Tuscany on such missions as the procurement of gangs of laborers for the work of cutting down the old towers and supplying their places with modern bastions able to resist artillery fire and to mount heavy guns. No smooth path was his, for the Pope vacillated. A major difficulty was the treatment of the fortifications south of the Arno (Letter no. 209). If a small area were encircled, many houses would need to be destroyed lest they give shelter to an enemy. If the area were extended, a large army would be required to man the walls. Should the hill of San Miniato be included? If it were, it could easily be made into a castle inaccessible from the city and yet dominating it, for the security of any tyrant—however unpopular—who might occupy it (Letter no. 210). Machiavelli was thinking of the castle in Forlì that Caterina Sforza held, and of that in Milan (*Prince* 20). The later Medici history of Florence justified his fears.

Even some rascally speculators in real estate were able to get the Pope's ear and delay vital decisions. The land included within an enlarged fortified circuit would, he asserted, increase in value 80,000 ducats. There was plausibility in this. Buildings within the walls, being relatively secure, were worth much more than those outside; if an attack threatened, intelligent defenders would embarrass the enemy by turning the country for a mile from the city walls into a desert (*Art of War,* bk 7). Yet Machiavelli does not believe that the city treasury could avail itself of the increased value, nor could it, except by means of a tax on the unearned increment. Even that increment would be only potential unless the population of the city grew sufficiently to cause a demand for the newly enclosed land, used earlier only for agriculture. We may recall that even north of the Arno there were uninhabited areas within the unnecessarily spacious walls until the nineteenth century. To a secretary interested in immediate defense, all dallying was hard to bear.

As in his early chancellorship, Machiavelli's devotion and ability expanded his duties far beyond the minimum. Though, as he wrote to Guicciardini, his head was full of bastions, he was also much occupied—inevitably to the neglect of the walls—with business relating to the army intended to defend Florence, and all Italy south of the Apennines from the imperial forces. This task was one at which he could labor with all his heart, knowing, as is hinted in *The Prince* 10, that a city is better defended by a proper army in the field than by walls. Such an army, however, could not be provided. The Secretary had the unhappiness of seeing all he had written (as in *The Prince* 12) on the ineffectiveness of hired soldiers borne out. The mercenary general Frederick of Urbino was unable or unwilling to accomplish anything. This Machiavelli sets forth in a letter to Cavalcanti (No. 219 B). From Forlì and Brisighella he writes to his old correspondent Vettori, full of zeal for Florence and belief that proper effort can repel the imperial army, for "if it did not encounter those who abandoned themselves, it would not capture a bake-oven" (No. 223); but self-abandonment, loss of courage, is fatal. In one of these letters the writer applies to himself what he had earlier asserted of Florentine patriots (*Hist. Flor.* 3.7): "I love my native city more than my own soul" (No. 225). Such is Machiavelli's devotion.

When he was absent from the city on army business, there was a revolution (16 May 1527) and a second expulsion of the Medici family. He was the servant of a nonexistent government. Once he had lost his place when the Medici returned; now he lost it when they fled. But he had no long time to regret that circumstances again prevented him from serving the city he loved, for on 22 June 1527 he died.

Machiavelli's life from 1512 until his death was no period of uninterrupted leisure for study and writing. Even in his first year of supposed retirement, he was often called upon to explain matters relating to the offices he had held. Yet as the years went on, he frequently did have months permitting him to give his chief attention to the *Discourses, The Art of War, Mandragola* and *The History of Florence*. Especially when we consider his last year, with public duties multiplied, we see why he made no further progress with the *History*. For one who was practical man as well as student, whose writing never was that of a cloistered scholar, periods of activity in the world would have been stimulating. From temporary employment he would have gone back to write—and to manage his farms—with higher hopes for the future. His career, therefore, need not be broken into two parts, though before 1512 he surely gave first attention to the duties of his office, and after 1512, until his last year, he had more leisure for writing. His behavior at Lucca, when on a mission there, may be taken as typical. Though carrying on his duties faithfully, he still found time for writing. When at Carpi on business he spent unoccupied time in reading (Letter no. 182). In 1504 he wrote the *First Decennale*; in 1509, while on a mission to North Italy, he wrote one-half of the *Second Decennale*. References within the poem *On Ambition* and its similarity to the official letters dispatched to Florence in 1509 indicate that it was composed at the same time. It appears, then, that Niccolò's life was always much of the same sort, with zealous attention to public duties when he had any laid upon him, yet also permitting sometimes more, sometimes less time for study, writing and pleasant association with friends.

❦ II ❧

The Mind of a Statesman and a Poet

"I LOVE my native city more than my own soul," said Machiavelli near the end of his life (Letter no. 225), taking for himself his earlier praise of Florentine patriots. Yet Florence did not always understand his love. The returning Medici supporters in 1512 could comprehend a party love, founded on self-interest. That Niccolò felt such party-love, after his long service with the republican government, the new rulers took for granted. He was expelled from office, confined to Tuscany, even tortured in prison. But however much he preferred the Florence of Soderini to that of Pope Leo, still—whatever the change in those who controlled her—the city was that Florence whom he delighted to serve. From factional advantage might come personal advancement, wealth. As the servant of all the people of Florence, even of the rocks built into her walls and her dwellings, Machiavelli remained poor. Of her, not of his own advantage, he had thought. That she was controlled at any moment by one group rather than another mattered to him in so far as that group agreed more or less with himself in putting first the good of the city as a whole. Only through favor with the Medici could he gain employment on Florentine business, yet for him such labor would have been not to advantage the Medici party but to benefit the city as a unit, her men and her materials, what he called her universality. Though Florence, as the smaller, more comprehensible entity, the one to which he was habituated, first and last engaged his attention, yet his devotion passed

43

over into regard for all Italy as his country. Other cities that he visited, Verona, Genoa, are his too. When for a few months he resided in Lucca, he acted as a Lucchese, interesting himself in her methods of government and writing a life of her hero, Castruccio Castracani, one of Florence's worst enemies. Never does he look at Castruccio with the eyes of a mere Florentine.

Through his devotion to Italy as a land, with her mountains and her shores, to Florence with her towers and her river, he the more clearly saw the defects of both. These he referred especially to division: hostile states, jealous factions, universal selfishness. Once for a moment he became a dreamer, in the last chapter of *The Prince* imagining a united Italy. Nowhere else does he suggest such union as likely or feasible; the influence against union of the Church's temporal power—to take an instance from *Discourses* 1.12—he clearly sees. France or Spain is in great measure unified, but not Italy. So striking is the last chapter of *The Prince* in its call for a union not warranted by immediate conditions that critics who have thought Niccolò impractical need not be rebuked. There he declares the time ripe for action, hoping too much from a Medici pope. But for the most part he looks at the past and present, without excursions into the future.

The Roman past he saw in bright colors, as may be excused to a life-long reader of Livy. The mediaeval past he did not make over-good, as the first book of *The History of Florence* testifies. Moreover, his position has been unconsciously distorted by students, prone to see black and white, without intermediate shades. Often he qualifies his praise of Rome, quite apart from lamenting that at last she too sunk under tyranny, having lost her virtue. Machiavelli's Rome begins with Romulus and continues through the Punic wars. Yet even this early Rome was imperfect. She had her internal troubles; her superiority was that she could deal with them as Florence could not. Her government, indeed, Machiavelli assigned to the best type, in which a mixture of elements gave recognition to the largest possible number of persons within the state. Thus stability was secured, enabling Rome to expand and to endure for a long period. Such was her policy in citizenship and military matters that she could grow with security. This Niccolò contrasted with the mistaken policy of Venice and Florence. Yet Rome fell. Even when Rome was virtuous her armies were defeated—defeated by a Carthaginian army made up partly of mercenary cavalry, the troops whom Machiavelli was disposed to consider least effective. So Rome herself was not completely admirable, though in an imperfect world her long life and marvelous achievement entitled her to respect for an example provided by no other city. Even superior Roman ways could not be taken over without examination, notwithstanding all Machiavelli's admiration. In the *Discourse on Remodeling the Government of Florence,* suggestion from Rome is indirect and limited to an attempt to give proper consideration to the various classes of inhabitants as they were considered in Livy's Rome. But the form of government is not Roman; it is what Florentines will accept as compatible with their experience.

Even in war, where the Romans so excelled, our author still looks at his own time, asking what from Roman practice is applicable. Essentially the answer is training, discipline. There is no slavery to detail. The long pikes Niccolò in *The Art of War* gave to many of his infantrymen were justified by the Greeks, not the Romans. (Actually he, like other Italians, borrowed them from the armory of the Swiss.) So, however much the Secretary admired Livy's Romans, he never made them an abstract ideal. Continually he asks himself: Will this Roman method fit Italian conditions at the moment when I write? And those Italian conditions are carefully and shrewdly observed.

Such limitation, implied rather than expressed, appears in much of his work. With respect to his most prominent achievement, *The Prince*, one cannot too often repeat that its purpose is limited. Its specific rather than far-reaching intention is in part dimmed by the author's essay-like manner of writing, which leads him discursively into matters not demanded by a rigid outline. The main theme—how a new prince makes his position firm—scarcely appears in such chapters as that on ecclesiastical princes, or on the successors of Alexander the Great. Machiavelli could easily have developed the principles of good government for the production of the common good. But he takes it for granted, concealing it behind his main preoccupation: the new prince making himself secure. Justice understood by a man who no longer is on the throne profits little those whom his successor rules. It is not strange that critics unused to Machiavelli's power to concentrate on a single matter directly under his eye have been puzzled by *The Prince*, and so have had recourse to ingenious explanations sometimes—for Machiavelli is imperfect as well as Protean —having some secondary relevance.

With his ability to avoid the abstract and remote and to look at the world as it is, without contaminating his analysis by intruding the world as it ought to be or as the application of some admirable code of ethics would make it, Machiavelli has confused readers seeking moral teaching. The usual reformer observes what is bad, searches his mind for a remedy, finds what he considers a solution. But too often into his new method creeps his unconscious assumption that while the old scheme has been run by men imperfect, even corrupt, his new one is to be conducted with perfect competence and absolute integrity. The teachers in his ideal reformed university, for example, are like angels. But Machiavelli lived in a world where men are fallible.

This he put strikingly, as though to rouse the opposition of any who believe in Man as perfect:

> As a usual thing this can be said about men: they are ungrateful, without firmness, pretenders and falsifiers; they run away from danger; they are eager for gain. As long as you benefit them, are entirely yours, they offer you their blood, their property, their lives, their children, as I said above, when need for them does not exist; but when need comes upon you, they do the opposite (*Prince* 17).

So true is this that a prince may find good works dangerous to him, making him hated,

> for when that large body, whether the common people, or the soldiers, or the nobility, by whose support you know you must keep yourself in your position, is corrupt, you must adapt yourself to its nature in order to please it. Then good works are evidently your enemies (*Prince* 19).

Only in a state wholly virtuous would good actions always be a ruler's friends.

On the nature of good actions Machiavelli is clear. In *The Art of War,* much of his concern is the difference between soldiers who are corrupt and those who are not. In *The Prince,* chap. 15, he distinguishes between how men live and how they ought to live. There too he says of his list of good qualities that a prince possessing such virtues would be worthy of the highest praise, but that human conditions prohibit the new ruler from practising them to the full. In the eighteenth chapter he makes plain that his prince is well aware of the demands of faith, charity, humanity, religion: when possible he will conform to them; only under necessity does he depart from them. Necessity comes from the wickedness of subjects and of hostile princes.

In his *Exhortation to Penitence,* Niccolò includes the

highest duties of man under charity or love, which is of more worth than all the other virtues. It is important to observe that the charitable man is willing to punish the wicked; the wise prince will do so when he can. It is not part of Machiavelli's ethics to condone wickedness or to allow the wicked to prey on the law-abiding without punishment. Such restraint of evildoers was part of the policy for which he commended Cesare Borgia in Romagna (*Prince* 7). Charity requires him who can to teach the ignorant and give advice to the erring. In the Preface of the *Discourses*, Machiavelli recognizes these functions as part of his own duty. Having a natural desire to do what will bring general benefit to all men, he undertakes this piece of writing for the instruction of kings, generals, citizens, lawgivers and others concerned for their countries. For light on Machiavelli's own character, we observe that the charitable man "endures his neighbors' defects." However much our author may advise prince and lawgiver to remember that men are generally wicked, however heartily he may deplore the selfishness that tore Florence into parties without regard for the common good, that took himself from his office and threw him into prison, he still is able to bear the defects and even the malice of humanity without complaint or rebellion. In the dedication of his *History of Florence,* he says that he "always avoided words full of hatred, as not required by the majesty and truth of history." Well he might have said that such words were not required by his own majestic and veracious spirit: he is not moved to hatred by the defects and evil deeds of his neighbors, however clearly he sees them. So he finds wickedness in the world and tolerates it, hoping for betterment. In his *Mandragola* he lets readers know that evil is being done, yet he is not shocked; so the world is constituted. He knows that his Prince, if he is to survive in a wicked world, must have prudence enough to be wicked, when necessary. Such is politics.

Thus understanding the world, Niccolò is not despairing or disillusioned. In *The History of Florence* he endeavors to teach Florentines and others that selfishness is the ruin of states. With no misgivings, though fully aware that man is naturally envious and resists new ideas, he labors on his *Discourses,* hoping that readers will find in his reflections something useful for their own lives. Sure that men are capable of disinterested service to their cities, he affirms it by the story of Michele da Lando (*Hist. Flor.* 3.17), whose qualities were "courage, prudence, goodness," without malice or ambition. What he could do for the "common good" of Florence he did, first of all by stopping robbery and house-burning. Taking hold of the Florentine government, Michele strove to better it by such specific actions as providing more representation for the poor. So act all of Machiavelli's reformers, beginning with Romulus.

Thus the Secretary never supinely accepts things as they are; he always hopes to see improvement. Of this longing for improvement the last chapter of *The Prince* provides the best-known proof. Another is his scheme for making Florence more of a republic by restoring the Great Council, part of his advice to the Medici tyrant. Yet on the other hand he felt that usually it is better to bear much bad government rather than to engage in conspiracy and strife with the hope of improvement, which is likely to be disappointing. This ability to stand firm, steadily attempting to do what he could, yet patiently accepting human fallibility, seeing all the fault and corruption of an administration—thus being in the city yet above it—is alone enough to evidence Machiavelli's great distance from such an abstraction as "the state," which has been foisted upon him by some who have not observed the deliberately restricted scope of the eighteenth chapter of *The Prince.* To him even such a word as *liberty* quickly becomes concrete, as "the power to enjoy unrestrained one's property without any fear, not to feel apprehension for the honor of one's women and children, not to have fears for oneself" (*Discourses* I.16). So little does he imagine man in bondage to "the state" that he sees the perfect government as that under which "every man can hold and defend whatever opinion he wishes" (*Discourses* I.10). Indeed for him the proper condition of man is one in which "it is not a sin to defend any opinion rationally, without trying to use either prestige or force" (*Discourses* I.17); indeed it is "good to reason about everything" (*Ibid.* I.18). Was ever a mind more tolerant and more expectant of toleration than that of the Florentine Secretary? But his is no passive intellect; it is ever alert. Formulas, even from the Romans, do not content it. To write *The Prince,* he departs entirely from those who have laid down rules for the conduct of kings, determining to follow the truth derived from actuality. Can such a freely ranging mind, responsible to itself alone, be bound by the tyrannizing concept of "the state"? An individual himself, he thinks of individuals; he is the author of a comic drama, *Mandragola,* in which each man has his own character.

Thus accustomed to facts, he developed not so much principles as specific views, derived from seeing how men act, maxims rather than a system, in freedom rather than rigidity. For example, he ends the third chapter of *The Prince:*

> We see by experience that the greatness in Italy of the Church and of the Spanish crown has been caused by the king of France, and his ruin has been caused by the first two. From this we get a general rule which never or seldom fails to apply: namely, that he who is the cause for the gain of power by anyone falls in ruin, because such power he brings about either with ingenuity or with force, and both of these are feared by him who has been made powerful.

His habit of observing (and he observed with great acuteness) is unlike that of the scientist. Indeed he is too much moved by his convictions to be scientific, to stand off and regard things as merely subjects of research. Even his impartiality is not cold but warm and interested. He can look at Pisa, the city he helped conquer, with such sympathy that one might think him a Pisan, not an aggressive Florentine. His lack of respect for mere data such as the number of mercenary soldiers killed at Zagonara or Anghiari is not carelessness; it is rooted in his strong objection to the mercenary spirit. This is not the attitude of a scientific historian. Machiavelli's power for detached observation is that of the artist, seeing with human interest and remembering in reflective leisure; to him men are men in all their complexity, to be regarded with charity, not as material for a scientist's conclusion. His is the poetical mind, seeing vividly and presenting dramatically.

When we remember how often, as Horace observed, poets have wished to benefit men in addition to pleasing them with imaginative creations, we understand Machiavelli's desire that the results distilled from his observation and study be useful, that his readers profit from the example of the Roman republic, the success and failure of Florentine policy, the men and women on the comic stage. Yet Machiavelli the artist, the poet, in *The Prince* and the *Discourses,* as well as in *Mandragola* and the verses on Ambition, is a poet with a difference, wearing the mask— indeed for some readers too effectively disguised—of historian and political observer. So the reader must needs be alert, for the more dispassionate Niccolò appears, the more poetical his words may become.

➥ III ➤

Thinking toward *The Prince*

(Letters nos. 124, 128, 131, 134)

So FAR as we know, *The Prince* was not begun until after
the letter of 26 August 1513; it was complete, though perhaps had not reached the form we now read, in December
1513. The letters here considered are almost preparatory
drafts for parts of it.

King Ferdinand of Spain, who dominates these letters, is
often mentioned in *The Prince*. The beginning of Chapter
21 is much like the latter part of the letter of 29 April;
some have thought the passage in the letter more spirited,
eloquent and poetic than the better-known one. In both,
Ferdinand is seen as essentially a new ruler who has raised
himself to a high place by his own abilities and efforts. Yet
Machiavelli feels that at times he has been unwise, especially in risking all of his kingdom without using all of
his forces. Such policy is condemned in *Discourses* 1.23,
perhaps written about the same time as the letter.

In *The Prince,* chap. 7, concerning Pope Julius II's enmity to Cesare Borgia, Machiavelli lays down as a certainty: "He who believes that recent favors make great men
forget old injuries, deceives himself." Cesare Borgia made
a mistake, therefore, in allowing the choice of Cardinal
San Piero ad Vincula as Pope Julius; "it was the cause of
his final ruin." In his letters Machiavelli looks at both sides
of this matter of forgetting old enmity. On 29 April 1513 he
wrote that the King of Spain would hardly join with the
King of France, "who presumably would remember old
injuries better than new favors." Yet on 10 August he

thought Ferdinand might win over the King of France, "for new benefits are wont to make men forget old injuries." King Ferdinand in his astuteness might be able to judge which result might follow, according to the circumstances.

For Ferdinand, Machiavelli felt some admiration, even though unwilling to allow him wisdom and disapproving of his morals, as shown in the King's persecution of the Moors (*Prince* 21). But his astuteness was such that the letter-writer could not believe that he would put himself in the power of the King of France, for "wise princes never put themselves, except through necessity, into the power of another man." Here, with a characteristic willingness to use the same word in varied senses, Machiavelli now seems to class Ferdinand among the wise, though he denied him that quality on 29 April 1513, allowing him to be only astute and lucky. Yet he makes the Spanish king clever enough to act so wisely that he will not put his fate in another's hands. In the chapter of *The Prince* outlining this King's brilliant career—with pity for his victims—we also read: "Wise princes with all their might avoid being in another's power" (Chap. 21).

In *The Prince*, chap. 12, looking at the military aspect of the Venetian power, and forgetting those instances in which they recovered by the peace-treaty what they lost by the war (see for example *History of Florence* 8.26), Machiavelli condemns the Venetian policy of hiring soldiers, declaring that their mercenaries lost them in one day, at Agnadello, what they had spent eight hundred years in building up. So on 26 August 1513, he writes that he had always thought their gain and retention of their empire a greater miracle than their loss of it. They had no generals and no soldiers of their own. Yet with all his bias against hired soldiers, Machiavelli admits that sometimes they succeed; in this very letter he indicates that Pyrrhus and Hannibal (mentioned in *Discourses*

3.21, as well as in *The Prince,* chap. 17) were successful with armies at least partly mercenary, because of their great ability. Italy, however, has not produced patriotic leaders; her ablest generals serve the French and the Spanish; we read in *The Prince:*

> In Italy there is no lack of material to which form could be given; there is great vigor in the limbs, if only it were not wanting in the heads. In duels and combats by a few warriors, Italians are superior in strength, skill, and cleverness, but when they are in armies, they do not compare [with foreigners]. This comes from the weakness of the leaders, because those who understand things are not obeyed, and every man thinks he understands, and up to now there has been no one who has been able to stand so high, through prudence and vigor, or through fortune, that the others will defer to him (chap. 26).

So on 26 August 1513 Machiavelli writes that he knows of no leader who can unite the Italians against the foreigners. Is it possible that he had changed his mind when in December he encouraged Giuliano and Lorenzo de'Medici to attempt Italian leadership (*Prince* 26)?

In *The Prince* the most elaborate figure of speech is that of the foreign invaders of Italy like a great flood covering the fertile fields (chap. 25). Yet in a dry season it is possible to dig ditches and build dikes so that the next flood will do no damage. So on 10 August 1513 Machiavelli wrote: "This German river is so large that it has need of a great dike to hold it . . . The precautions against this flood need to be taken now, before the Swiss put down roots in this land, and begin to taste the sweetness of ruling." In the informal letter another figure follows that of the flood.

To the diligent reader yet other signs will appear of the process by which a few months later Machiavelli came to *The Prince.*

Three Political Letters

(Nos. 145, 154, 155)

IN EARLIER letters to Vettori, Machiavelli appears as meditating on *The Prince;* in these he uses some of its principles soon after they were put in writing. High among his chief concerns are the Swiss. Of them Machiavelli had what we now think unduly great fear, founded on admiration of their military organization and comparison of them with the Romans. In spite of his belief in individual *virtù*, it did not occur to him that the Swiss failed to develop conspicuous leaders. Not then was there any Swiss statesman capable of planning and carrying out such a foreign policy as Machiavelli imagined. What he says in these letters is developed from a single sentence in *The Prince:* "The Swiss are heavily armed and perfectly free" (Chap. 12). In his *Discourses,* not far from the date of these letters, he speaks of them as "the teachers of the modern wars" (2.17).

Neutrality as treated in these letters is expanded with examples from *The Prince,* chap. 21, the Pope appearing as a temporal ruler, in the position of a lesser power between two stronger ones, namely France with her allies, and Spain with her allies; a third danger came from the Swiss. With one of the powerful the Pope must join, lest he cause both to hate him. Even if the side he chooses is defeated, its support continues to have value. In a defeated France, for example, he could take refuge at Avignon, still his property, where various popes lived, and have the support of a country so rich as to be in itself a "papacy." Moreover, the fortune of the victor may be "resurgent," to adapt the word used both in *The Prince* and the first letter of 20 Dec. 1514. In his long debate on the proper choice for the Pope in his unpleasant situation, Machiavelli is developing a passage in *The Prince*: "It is in the order of things that one never succeeds in escaping one affliction without running into another; prudence consists in recognizing the nature of the various afflictions and taking the least bad as something good" (chap. 21). This Pope Leo X must attempt to do.

In discussing what Henry VIII of England and the other kings will do, Machiavelli is not troubled by what the people think, remarking that they wish what the kings wish (20 Dec. 1514, no. 1). Thus he varies his statement of the power of the king's example (*Prince* 24, *Discourses* 3.29). In the same letter, too, he discusses the holding of mountain passes by the defenders of an invaded country, who by so doing would risk everything without using their entire forces (*Discourses* 1.23). Under the influence of his discussion of the Emperor Maximilian I as one who did not know his own mind (*Prince* 23), Machiavelli briefly says here: "I do not know what he will do at any time."

⊱ V ⊰

Savonarola

(Letter no. 3)

IN THIS letter we have Machiavelli at twenty-eight observing some striking public events in Florence: Savonarola's sermons. Here, as in other familiar letters not intended for publication, Machiavelli may be supposed to speak with less care than when expecting a wide audience. Yet even so he exhibits the same power to observe without passion that appears in much of his later writing. His own opinion is clear; he does not trust the preacher, though fascinated by his procedure and admiring his skill. The Frate, however, is to him more partisan than reformer. Apparently this opinion remained with him. In the *Discourses* he deals with Savonarola's law permitting men accused of political crime to appeal to the people. Its passage the Frate secured with great difficulty. Soon after its enactment, the right of appeal was refused to five citizens. Says Machiavelli:

> This deprived the Frate of more good reputation than any other happening, because if that law of appeal was useful, he should have had it observed; if it was not useful, he should not have had it passed. This event was the more noticed because the Frate in all the sermons he preached after the breaking of the law never either condemned those who broke it or excused their action, as though he did not wish to condemn it, as something to his advantage, and yet could not excuse it. By revealing his ambitious and partisan spirit, this conduct took reputation away from him and brought on him much reproach (1.45).

To Machiavelli, mourning (like Dante) over the internecine struggles of his native city, no man was so odious as the partisan, contrasted in his selfishness with Michele da Lando in his love for the town as a unity. Further, Machiavelli held that Savonarola as churchman and moralist had failed to apply the prudence that appeared in his writings. Remarking on the Italian military failure that made so easy Charles VIII's march through the peninsula, he adds: "He who said that our sins caused it told the truth; but they were not the sins he believed they were, but those I have been telling about; and because they were sins by the princes, the princes have paid the penalty for them" (*Prince* 12). With this comment on Savonarola, for an instant we are in the atmosphere of *Mandragola*. Frate Timoteo's parishioner asks: "Do you think the Turk will come into Italy this year?" to be answered: "If you don't pray, he will" (3.3). Machiavelli could praise a Numa-like simulation for political purposes, but still demanded rational connection of cause and effect, rejecting the procedures of the popular evangelist and of the politician seeking emotional support.

In a comic letter of 17 May 1521 (no. 179) on a preacher for Florence, Machiavelli speaks of Fra Girolamo as *versuto*, with an obvious bad meaning, such as crafty or even malicious, since the Dominican is contrasted with the perfect preacher, prudent, blameless and true, whom Machiavelli's friends desire him to engage for a course of sermons in Florence. A comic reference also occurs in one of the texts of the *Andria* translated. Terence makes his slave say: "Davos sum, non Oedipus." In his desire to turn the Latin into vivid Italian, Machiavelli renders this, according to an autograph manuscript: "Io son Davo, non profeta, ut non el frate" (1.2). That is, "I am Davus, not a prophet, since not the Frate." One is tempted, on the basis of such a hint of Savonarola, to suppose that the words *el frate,* as in the letter of 1497-98, mark the version of the *Andria* as of about that date. At any rate, in both writings the prophetic power of the Frate is not taken seriously.

Elsewhere the preacher appears better, for *The Prince* makes him the "unarmed prophet" (chap. 6) unable to use force when the people no longer can be swayed by his eloquence. In this passage the other examples given are Moses, Cyrus, Theseus and Romulus, all men whom the Secretary admired, as is evident in *Prince* 6 and 26 and in the *Discourses* 1.2, 9). The new laws (*ordini nuovi*) of Savonarola are good provisions, as in *Discourses* 1.9, where the reformer is to order the state anew, remodeling it with complete change of its old laws (*ordini*). In *Discourses* 3.30, Moses again appears as severely enforcing his new laws and *ordini*. Along with him appears not only Savonarola but Piero Soderini, whose regime Machiavelli so long served and supported, with general approval, even though Soderini failed at last. Machiavelli says also that Savonarola recognized the necessity of force but did not succeed in communicating his prudent observation to his followers, who had power to compel obedience to his new measures.

In two passages, Niccolò says something in direct commendation:

> The people of Florence were persuaded by Frate Girolamo Savonarola that he was speaking with God. I am not going to decide whether it was true or not, because of so great a man we ought to speak with reverence. But I do say that multitudes believed him, without seeing anything unusual to make them believe, because his life, his learning, the subject he took, were enough to get him their belief (*Discourses* 1.11).

In the context appears as a parallel the Roman king Numa, whose methods, even to his pretence that he was advised by a nymph to prepare new *ordini* for Rome, were approved by the writer. Numa was superior to Fra Girolamo in that he was able to give his plan permanence. Even more favorably, Machiavelli asserts that Savonarola's writings show "his learning, his prudence, and the vigor of his intellect" (*Discourses* 1.45). This is in harmony with praise by Guicciardini (*Hist. Flor.* 16), who also accuses Fra Girolamo of pride and ambition. To read Savonarola's political writings without remarking passages that would have pleased the Secretary is impossible. Machiavelli's prescription for Florentine government in his work *On Remodeling the Government of Florence* seemingly owes much to the Frate.

In his verse account of ten years of Florentine history, *The First Decennale,* Machiavelli writes:

> That which to many was displeasing and made you [the Florentines] abandon union was that sect under whose emblem your city lay. I mean of that great Savonarola, who, inspired with vigor divine, kept you enchained with his words. But because many feared to see little by little the ruin of their city under his prophetic teaching, no place in which to reunite you could be found, if his divine light did not increase or if it was not extinguished with a greater fire (154-165).

However brief, this is a systematic account written some six years after the event, and for its own sake; it is not incidental or illustrative. That Machiavelli did not live to write for his *History of Florence* on the years of Fra Girolamo's activity we must always regret. There are, however, brief and scattered notes for sections on the Frate. They indicate narratives of the disturbances raised by his friends and his enemies, and some lively accounts of his preaching and his power—so great that foreigners mocked Florentines by saying that they had escaped from the hands of the Medici and fallen into the Frate's. One note reports Savonarola's interview with King Charles VIII of France at Poggibonsi in June 1495, where he is said to have "talked the father of the leek" to the King. This fits with the Frate's own report that he spoke *"modestamente ma vivo"* (modestly but vigorously) if we allow the last word to cover prophetic threats. Francesco Guicciardini writes:

> Girolamo Savonarola, mixing with his words, according to his custom, the divine authority and name, exhorted the King with the greatest vigor to return the cities [which he had taken] to the Florentines, adding to his persuasions the most serious threats that if he did not observe what he had sworn with such solemnity (touching the Gospels with his hand as though before God's eyes), he would without delay be severely punished by God (*Hist. Italy*, bk 2, year 1495).

In Machiavelli's notes there is no indication of comment on the Frate's political theories, such as might have appeared in the *History of Florence*, yet since we have only chronological jottings, silence means nothing.

It appears that Machiavelli retained the opinions he hints at rather than expresses in his letter reporting Savonarola's sermons. Though realizing the Frate's capacity as a political thinker and practical statesman, he deplored his partisan violence, his egotism, his reliance on histrionic effect, his mixture of the ecclesiastical with the political. At their best, Savonarola's political theories and actions entitled him to stand as a fifth statesman in the company of Moses, Romulus, Theseus and Cyrus, but his failure in the vigor and wisdom required for bringing his ideas to fruition placed him among the unsuccessful with Cesare Borgia and Piero Soderini.

❧ VI ❧

Machiavelli and the Poets

(Letters 120, 122, 137, 152, 159, 166, 199, 200, 206)

WRITING of his life at Sant'Andrea in Percussina, Machiavelli says that after observing his wood-cutters, he went
on to his aviary (Letter no. 137). There he took from his
pocket a book, "either Dante or Petrarch or one of the
lesser poets, such as Tibullus or Ovid." He read of their
tender passions and their loves, remembered his own,
dreamed for a while. Then he went on to the tavern where
he met various men and noted their various tastes and
fancies. In the evening he read such authors as Livy and
Tacitus. A part of the day for poetry is characteristic of
Niccolò. How otherwise could he have concluded *The
Prince* with a quotation from Petrarch? Yes, and the
Exhortation to Penitence in the same way? Petrarch seems
to have been a favorite; indeed this very letter opens with
a quotation from *The Triumph of Eternity*. Through reading Petrarch's *Triumphs* as well as Dante's verse, he acquired such command of the *terza rima* as appears in his
Capitoli and in *The [Golden] Ass*. In Letter 122 he uses
lines from Petrarch with a deliberate adaptation to his
own feeling. Another letter (no. 159) he begins with a
sonnet that makes him one of the followers of Laura's
poet.

Dante often occurs to him also, as when he quotes to
express the fears raised in him by a letter of Vettori's (no.
120). Writing to Guicciardini, he cites a passage on the
sufferings of Pope Boniface at the hands of soldiers as a
parallel to the troubles of Pope Clement VII (no. 199).

Though he says to his friend, "You know the verses; read the rest for yourself," Guicciardini did not know them and had difficulty in finding a copy of Dante in Romagna. At last he succeeded, but the volume offered no explanatory note. He thinks the quotation one of those things of which Niccolò "always has his sleeves full," that is, things that he knows and other men do not. In his next letter from Machiavelli he met another quotation from the *Commedia*, on the marriages arranged by Romeo for the daughters of the duke of Provence (no. 200). Machiavelli's most amusing use of Dante is in his comic epitaph for Piero Soderini, quoted above in the section on his life.

From Ovid, Machiavelli often draws, as when he quotes from the *Metamorphoses* for Vettori (Letter no. 159). Earlier he quoted a bit which he expected his friend to recognize and continue (Letter no. 152).

In his *Clizia*, in a passage not found in his source, Plautus' *Casina*, Machiavelli writes:

Certainly he who said that the lover and the soldier are alike told the truth. The captain wants young men as soldiers; women don't want their lovers to be old. It is a horrid thing to see an old man enlisted as a soldier; it is very horrid to see him in love. Soldiers fear the anger of the captains; lovers fear not less that of their mistresses. Soldiers sleep on the ground out-of-doors; lovers on the ledges of the house-walls. Soldiers pursue their enemies to the death; lovers their rivals. Soldiers in the darkness of night when the winter is coldest march through the mud, exposed to rain and wind, to carry through an enterprise that will make them gain a victory; lovers in like ways, and with like and greater hardships, strive to gain their beloved. In the same way in warfare and in love, secrecy, fidelity and courage are needed; the dangers are the same, and generally the end is the same. The soldier dies in a ditch; the lover dies in despair (1.2).

The speaker mentioned is Ovid. Machiavelli has adapted to prose the following passage:

Every lover goes to war, and Cupid has his camp. Take my word for it, Atticus, every lover goes to war. The age that is suited for war is also fit for Venus. Horrid is an aged soldier; horrid is aged love. The spirit that captains want in a strong soldier, the fair girl wants in the man who is to be with her. Both keep awake all night; both sleep on the ground—one guarding his mistress' door; the other his captain's. Long is the road of the soldier's duty; send the girl ahead, the vigorous lover follows endlessly. He will go upon difficult mountains and into rivers doubled by cloudbursts, he will tread the drifted snows. When he is to embark upon the sea, he will not chatter of threatening East Wind, nor will he ask for favoring stars before putting his oar in the water. Who but a soldier or a lover will bear the chill of night and the snow mingled with heavy rain? One as a scout is sent against dangerous enemies; the other keeps his eye on his rival as an enemy. The first besieges strong towns; the second the door of his cruel love. One smashes doors; the other city-gates (*Amores* 1.9).

Ovid develops the parallel further, with classical illustration Machiavelli felt unsuited for such a comedy as *Clizia*. He has adapted it to Florentine life, in the references to the ledges where the lover sleeps. Machiavellian is the reference to secrecy, fidelity, courage; for satire Machiavelli adds how soldier and lover die.

In comedy Niccolò even imitated Catullus, as did Ben Jonson in his *New Inn* 5.2. Callimaco's passion he expresses in *Mandragola* thus:

In every limb so great a desire to be once with her attacks me that from the soles of my feet to my head I feel myself overcome. My legs tremble, my vitals are in commotion; my heart is uprooted from my breast; my arms lose their vigor; my tongue grows silent; my eyes are dazzled; my brain whirls (4.1).

Catullus, inspired by Sappho, wrote *Ad Lesbiam, to Lesbia:*

My senses are snatched away, for as soon as I see you,

Lesbia, I have in my mouth no sound of voice, my tongue falters, a subtle flame flows down my body, my ears ring with inward chiming, both my eyes are covered with darkness (51).

Machiavelli's imitation, with its touch from Petrarch (*Sonnet* 134), is exaggerated for comic effect.

Writing to Lodovico Alamanni, he tells of his pleasure in reading the latest contemporary poem, Ariosto's *Orlando Furioso* (Letter no. 166). Perhaps he had in mind Ariosto's description of Cairo (15.63) when he used the name to signify a city of enormous size (Letter no. 206). In Letter 159 he quotes from another romantic poem, Pulci's *Morgante*.

Altogether the letters show Machiavelli conversant with much poetry and assuming that his friends will recognize his references to it. We need not be astonished when in his political works he quotes from Juvenal or from a drama by Lorenzo the Magnificent.

⊰ VII ⊱

Florentine Marriages

(Letters no. 146, 167, 168, 196, 199, 200, 211)

GIOVANNI VERNACCI, his nephew, beginning commercial life as a Florentine business-man in the Levant, was often in Niccolò's mind. Thinking on his financial advancement, the uncle in 1514 suggested a marriage (Letter no. 146). He knew of a very rich artisan who had sufficiently risen in the social scale to be among those eligible for office in Florence. He had a daughter somewhat lame, but otherwise handsome, good and worthy. With her a marriage could be arranged by which the father would give a dower of two thousand sealed florins, and open a shop in the wool business which Giovanni could manage. The suggestion reflects Machiavelli's financial situation and perhaps his discouragement at that time. At least he is willing to see his nephew marry into a family of lower social station than his own for the sake of only a small sum of money, and to take a wife whose lameness would render her father more than usually anxious about her marriage. Obviously nothing came of the suggestion, for in letters on 5 January and 25 January 1517-18 Machiavelli brings up the topic anew.

A few years later he became involved in the marriage negotiations for the eldest daughter of Francesco Guicciardini. This friend, from a family of such standing that no member of the Florentine aristocracy could object to its social position, had four daughters. Thus he realized keenly the condition of which Dante's Cacciaguida spoke, praising the manners of a time when

66

the daughter at her birth did not rouse fear in her father, because the time and the dower did not flee from right measure in either direction (*Paradiso* 15.103).

That is, the age for marriage was not very low, and, even more, the demands for dower were not excessive. With four daughters, Guicciardini's fear was four times multiplied, since he was not a very wealthy man. Even his favor with the Medici Pope, Clement VII, and his important position in the Pope's employ were not enough to secure for his first daughter such a marriage as he desired, unless he paid a dower beyond his means. Niccolò did all he could to aid him, by attempting discreet negotiations with Florentines having eligible sons, and by giving advice. One suggestion was that great effort be made to secure for the first daughter a marriage into a wealthy and influential family. Then it was likely that the others could make good marriages on smaller provisions, since possible husbands would reckon on the value of a connection with the husband of the first. Florentine notions of family responsibility made such advice worth regarding. In Niccolò's *Belfagor* the devil of that name, disguised as a Florentine business-man, is urged by his wife until he sets all her brothers up in business, where they lose the property he has entrusted to them.

As a means for raising the desirable sum, Machiavelli would have his friend apply to Pope Clement VII for a supplement to what he could himself afford to offer to a son-in-law. This procedure he justifies by the example of other Florentines of high position who are richer than Guicciardini and whose services to the Medici family have been less important than his. He outlines the arguments Guicciardini should use and even more insists on the way he should ask, in a fashion that reminds one of analyses of human conduct in *The Prince:*

The whole thing consists in asking boldly and showing great discontent if you do not receive. And princes easily bend themselves to do new favors for those for whom they have done old ones, or rather they are so afraid of losing, if they refuse, the benefits of their earlier favors, that they hasten to confer new ones (Letter no. 199).

This is a method for forcing an imprudent prince to act like a wise one in conferring on his officers, in recognition of ability and faithfulness, such benefits as Machiavelli in *Prince* 22 says are bestowed by the virtuous ruler.

Machiavelli the Comic Observer

(Letters no. 3, 122, 137, 138, 140, 142, 144, 182, 183)

How DO men act? was Machiavelli's constant question, and one of his chief pleasures was in mingling with them. His observation of their tastes and fancies was taken into the stores of his experience and emerged in his comic writings indeed, but also in the matured consideration of his *History of Florence*. Francesco Guicciardini was amused at his friend's position as ambassador to the Franciscans, but Machiavelli accepted it, signing himself in formal Latin: "Orator pro Republica Florentina ad Fratres minores" (Letter no. 182). Even the notion that he could gain proft there for his *History of Florence* he jocosely accepted from Guicciardini, saying that he had lost nothing by coming to this republic of wooden sandals, because he had learned of many of their regulations that had good in them; these he could often use in his *History*, especially in comparisons, "because when I need to speak of silence I can say: 'They are quieter than the friars when they are eating'" (Letter no. 183). Under the joking there is truth. Niccolò's study was mankind, and he profited from all he met. So in his exile at Sant'Andrea in Percussina he did not sink into listlessness but kept his brain from moulding by association with the villagers, "from whom he learned a variety of things, and noted the various tastes and diverse fancies of men" (Letter no. 137).

Such power to observe men's humors, without allowing any personal feeling to ruin perspective, we observe in his letter describing his visit to Savonarola's preaching (no. 3). That letter illuminates his account of a Franciscan preaching at Santa Croce, whom he did not hear, "because I don't frequent such doings"; but his amusement at the imposter and at all Florence excited about the two million devils unchained to bring about the marvels prophesied by the half-hermit, rests on his observation of conduct (No. 138).

Trivial incidents gain larger life under Machiavelli's eyes. There is the stingy Tommaso who bought seven pounds of veal, then was alarmed at its price and looked for help in bearing the cost. Machiavelli and others joined him at dinner and we may be sure had an amusing time. When the shares were figured, the impecunious Niccolò lacked four soldi of his share. The miserly Tommaso has several times dunned him for the money, once on the Ponte Vecchio. Knowing that this is something of a joke on his own financial habits, Machiavelli remarks: "I don't know that you will think him wrong" (No. 122).

Told at greater length is the story of the discomfiture of Giuliano Brancacci, a Florentine rascal (No. 144). First it is put as though he went out hunting for "birds," that is, for compliant homosexuals. Searching the nooks and crannies of central Florence, at last he found a boy who pleased him. Learning that his name was Michele, he then said: "I am Filippo da Casavecchia. If you come or send to my shop tomorrow, I shall content you." So in the morning the boy sent for his money. The astonished Filippo refused to pay, and summoned Michele. He appeared, rebuked Filippo, and threatened that if he were cheated he would bring disgrace on Filippo. The latter, however, stood his ground, saying he was not a man who meddled with such rascality, and that the boy had better attempt to find out who had tricked him rather than attack Filippo without cause; he told Michele to come again the next day. Puzzled, the boy accepted this. Filippo was then at his wit's end, and his resolution wavered like the water in the mouth of the Arno at Pisa in a north wind. If he paid a florin, he would become the boy's vineyard, making himself guilty; if he denied it without learning the truth, Michele would be believed; if he was mistaken in selecting the real culprit, he would make an enemy and still would be thought guilty. At last he selected Brancaccio, who had tricked him once before, as the rascal. So then he went to Alberto Lotti, one of Michele's relatives, for help. Alberto, examining the boy, said to him: "Would you recognize the voice of the man who said he was Filippo?" Since Michele thought he would, Alberto took him to Santo Ilario, where Brancaccio spent much of his time. There they found him in the middle of a crowd telling stories, and came up behind him until they heard him speaking. Just then Brancaccio turned and, seeing them, was embarrassed and made off. The truth was plain. So in the Carnival people ask: "Are you Brancaccio or are you Casa?" In this story Machiavelli is not disturbed by his characters, such as Florence and others cities abounded in, yet he does not palliate them. "The boy," he says, "was bad rather than merely of little account." Yet the comparison to the bird-catcher is amusing, even the innocent Filippo is comic in his embarrassment, and the discomfiture of the rascal is accomplished without a word. Finally the Florentines who savor the joke are comic as they all repeat the formula.

Both Filippo Casavecchio and Brancaccio appear when not at odds in an earlier letter of comment on Vettori's own account of an evening at his house in Rome (No. 142). The whole scene is imagined by Machiavelli with a vividness and appreciation of folly not to be surpassed. Vettori himself—Florentine ambassador to the Pope and a man through whose influence Machiavelli was hoping for government employment—is subdued to a low bourgeois level. The scene does indeed fit with Machiavelli's discussion of the levity permitted to the grave man off duty, who being held wise by day will never be thought foolish by night (No. 140). This idea he repeated as one of the sayings he later attributed to his fictitious Castruccio Castracani:

> One night when he was in the house of one of his gentlemen, where many ladies were gathered for entertainment, he danced and had a good time more than suited his station. But when one of his friends rebuked him, he said: "He who is thought wise by day will never be thought crazy by night.

After praising the prudence, eloquence, keen mind, and power to execute that made Lorenzo the Magnificent known far beyond the bounds of Italy, Machiavelli continued:

> We cannot mention any vices that spotted such great virtues, though he was much involved in the affairs of Venus, and took delight in comic and satirical men, and in puerile sports, more than seemed suitable to so great a man, so that many times he was seen with his sons and daughters, taking part in their childish sports (*Hist. Flor.* 8.36).

Machiavelli's praise of folly is wholly ingenuous, directed against the wisdom which is wise only in its own conceit and which lacks touch with reality.

Machiavelli's high exertion contrasted with his share in life's triviality appears in the most famous of the letters, announcing the composition of *The Prince* (Letter no. 137). In the background are the illiterate inhabitants of a tiny village. Early in the morning Niccolò goes out to observe men cutting wood on his farm—thus imitating his father's careful husbandry. Here he listens to the bad-luck stories these workmen always had ready, either about themselves or about their neighbors. Then comes his dealing with Florentines who bought some of his wood, where vexation passes into amusement:

Frosino da Panzano sent for a number of cords of wood without saying a thing to me, and on payment he wanted to keep back from me ten lire, which he says he should have had from me four years ago, when he beat me at *cricca* at Antonio Guicciardini's. I raised the devil and was going to prosecute as a thief the waggoner who had come there for the wood, but Giovanni Machiavelli came between us and got us to agree.

Then he tells the story of the stingy man who with the help of his wife, children, and servants piled up the cord sent him so tight, beating the sticks down into crevices between others, that it turned out only half a cord. If this man in his stinginess was a comic cheater, Niccolò knew that there was possible comedy on his side, in that his laborers might have piled the wood so loosely that they cheated by making less than a cord into a cord. Mark Twain in the days when Mississippi steamers burned wood under their boilers speaks of wood for sale that was "piled by them cheats so you can throw a dog through it anywheres" (*Huckleberry Finn,* chap. 19). An even more exaggerated story comes from early days in Western New York. A widow bought a cord of wood from a farmer who delivered it on a bob-sled drawn by two horses. He drove into her narrow yard and piled the wood, very loosely, under her disapproving eyes. When he had finished, he remarked that he hadn't left much space for turning his horses and sled, to get out of the yard. The widow answered: "Drive right through the holes in the woodpile." Doubtless Vettori, who received the letter, had heard such stories. Dismayed by his dealings with skin-flints, Machiavelli gave up selling wood, saying he had no more, but even then he could not escape comic troubles. Batista Guicciardini, who had agreed to take a cord, made so much of his disappointment as to count it among his misfortunes at Prato. Batista was *podestà* in the city when she was captured and horribly sacked by the Spanish army less than a year and a half before, so that he suffered severely. His complaints exemplify the comedy depending on magnifying the trivial to make it appear of great consequence.

From the woodlot, Machiavelli passes on to his aviary, where he sits in the company of Dante, Petrarch, Ovid or Tibullus. In contrast, he goes to the inn, where he talks with the villagers, asks news from passers-by, and notes the various tastes and different fancies of men. So in the midst of trifles Niccolò is not merely a trifler; he is also the comic poet, the political philosopher in touch with fundamentals. Though when he wrote on politics he dealt with kings, he did not forget that the purpose of government is the good of the whole population, of which the most numerous part was such as the men and women he talked with in front of the inn at Sant'Andrea in Percussina.

After dinner, Machiavelli goes back to the inn, to meet more of those for whom princes exist, described in one of the oft-quoted passages of this letter. The working-day must be over, or the scene is exceptional, for in addition to the host he meets men who have their occupations, a butcher, a miller, two bakers.

> With these I sink into vulgarity for the whole day, playing at *cricca* and at trich-trach, and then these games bring on a thousand disputes and countless insults with offensive words, and usually we are fighting over a penny, and nevertheless we are heard shouting as far as San Casciano. So, involved in these trifles, I keep my brain from growing mouldy, and satisfy the malice of this fate of mine, being glad to have her drive me along this road, to see if she will be ashamed of it.

Even here the observing eye is alert and the mind is at work on—finally—the mystery of life, and on that fate, or here he might have said Fortune (as in the dedication of *The Prince*), that has him in her power.

Then at night a further contrast. With a brain free from mould, he goes in to the presence of the great, with whom for four hours he converses on the problem of man in society, and on his relation to the powerful whose conduct so greatly concerns the lowly. In this atmosphere, so close to the comedy of daily life, so remote from it, he composes *The Prince*. Fresh from reality, he is the surer in his defence of ideas that most writers attack, for, as he declares,

> I do not judge nor will I ever judge it a sin to make a rational defense of any opinion, without trying to use either authority or force (*Discourses* 1.58).

If it is true that the best explanation of comedy is to be found in incongruity, in contrast, Niccolò's day has enough of it to be a picture of the comic world. Whatever the lesser comic discords, the final incongruity is between the rational and the irrational, between man at the full development of his intellect, such as Dante planned for in *De Monarchia*, and man who fails to use his mind, that is, man who falls short of the best humanity, for whatever reason, whether excessive piety, excessive devotion to a cause, selfishness financial or intellectual, or lack of charity. Machiavelli may have spent a good deal of time playing *cricca* and other silly games, he may not have managed his property carefully, he couldn't get rich, yet in his most careless moods he still had the open and active perception, the interest in observing humble life, with all its defects, and the conduct of the mighty, with its failures, as one who trusted nevertheless in the high possibilities of the human mind. Yet he never went forth merely to observe, as does the scientist. He played trich-trach heartily and laughed at poor jokes because they amused him, as Shakespeare saw fun in the poor jokes he put in his plays. Both artists could laugh at the bawdry that has shocked their dignified biographers. So Machiavelli's observation came later than his experience, since it was the poet's distillation of what he saw, quite unlike the immediate findings of the scientist. Thus Machiavelli's sense of comedy passed into the wisdom of his writings and into his power to regard all men with charity.

Notes on Individual Letters

Some Personal Letters

(Nos. 117, 119, 120, 125, 129, 137, 142, 144, 145, 148, 159, 166, 167, 179, 182, 183, 186, 192, 196, 198, 199, 200, 204, 211, 222)

THE letter of 14 March 1512-13 (No. 117) was written after Machiavelli's sojourn in prison, because suspected of a plot against the Medici government. In this and the next letter (No. 119) he refers to a subject that was to engage him for a long time: his hope for suitable employment in Florence or elsewhere. Yet he does not lose courage: "I was born poor and learned earlier to stint myself than to prosper." In about three weeks comes his only prose mention of the torture of the rack, not put in the language of one asking sympathy. Possibly he was not severely tortured; at least he does not dwell on his afflictions. With good knowledge of his own temperament, he writes:

> Fortune has determined that since I don't know how to talk about the silk business or the wool business, or about profits and losses, I must talk about the government and I am obliged either to make a vow of silence or to discuss that.

Under all circumstances he was fascinated by the conduct of men in their organizations. The letters immediately following chiefly show what he called his "passion for politics," though two (Nos. 125, 129) are to his nephew in the Levant, for whom he felt great affection. He tells with brevity of his troubles, including danger of death. Yet he is so alert to his nephew's welfare as to advise him on writing letters of business: he is to tell too much rather than too little.

On 10 December 1513 comes the best-known of Machia-velli's letters (No. 137) indicated as having been written in Florence. Though important for its information about *The Prince*, it is also one of the fullest on his private life, giving an account of a day on his farm at Sant'Andrea in Percussina. He tells on the one hand of his reading in Latin and Italian poets (the only passage of its sort) and on the other of the vulgar company he sees at the inn; yet by associating with these workingmen he keeps his brain from getting mouldy. By contrast, in the evening he goes into his study where he meets the famous men of old, with whom he converses for four hours, while he feels no bore-dom; he forgets all his troubles; he does not dread poverty; death does not frighten him. In this retreat for the mind from the ills of life, he has composed a little book *On Princedoms,* which he is still enlarging and thoroughly revising.

His correspondent, Vettori, wishes him to give up his life in the country and go to Rome. Explaining why he cannot come, Machiavelli gets amusement from his hard situation. The Soderini are in Rome; he could not avoid seeing them, but such a meeting would cause suspicion in the Medici government, which is touchy and doubtful, as all new governments are. So he would on his return dis-mount not at his house but at the Bargello, the city jail. He continues with what seems a joking reference to a Florentine apparently known to Vettori; the passage, how-ever, is not now clear. Then, serious again, he says that if he had any opportunity to show the Medici what he can do, he is sure he would get permanent employment. If they will read his little book, they will see that he has not been asleep during his years as secretary. He insists on his honesty and goodness: "A man who has been honest and good for forty-three years, as I have, cannot change his nature; as a witness to my honesty and goodness, I have my poverty." Machiavelli knew the meaning of the word *goodness;* in this frank and unguarded letter, intended for the eyes of a friend, he could claim it for himself.

Other letters to Vettori show power for enjoyment of the comic, such as No. 144, incomparable in its presentation of low life in a not very moral Florence. There is also the letter (No. 159) in which he contrasts the two aspects in which he and his friend appear, sometimes as grave men thinking only of high matters full of honor and magnificence, then light-minded, inconstant, lascivious, concerned with trifles. Thus they imitate variable Nature. If some letters, those on Italian politics, have shown one side, and others, as Machiavelli's imaginative and dramatic picture of Vettori off duty at home (No. 142), show a different side, now he will combine them in one letter.

On his finances Machiavelli makes a plain statement (No. 145). Though his income is ninety florins or less, his taxes run to forty florins. Thus only fifty florins—presumably the income from his land—are left for the expenses of the family. What would be the equivalent of this sum at present, who can say? Machiavelli's salary as chancellor had been two hundred sealed florins, equal to about one hundred thirty-three gold florins. His friend Donato del Corno, who often appears in the letters to Vettori, lent Giuliano de' Medici five hundred florins. A large dower for Guicciardini's daughter was six thousand florins, a hundred and twenty times Machiavelli's annual income. Even if we suppose that much of the food for his family came from the farm, available funds were small. From his *Book of Records* we infer that Niccolò's father, Bernardo, economical and painstaking, derived more from the land than did his son, so that he could live frugally on his hereditary income. But Niccolò had grown accustomed to thinking of such income as only a supplement to his salary, and his temperament was different:

79

I am using up my money, and I see, if God does not show himself more favorable to me, that I shall be one day forced to leave home and hire out as a tutor or a secretary to a constable,[1] since I can do nothing else, or fix myself in some desert land to teach reading to boys, and leave my family here, which could reckon that I am dead, and would get on much better without me, because I am an expense to them, being used to spending, and unable to get on without spending (No. 148).

In December 1517 Niccolò is in a happier frame of mind, writing from Florence and planning a trip to France, as though his income had improved (No. 166). In January, however, he warns his nephew that he is without influence to aid him (No. 167). Three years later he writes on his nephew's legal troubles in Florence as the result of his absence in the Levant (No. 169).

In May 1521, on his mission to the Minor Friars at Carpi, Machiavelli wrote to Francesco Guicciardini, papal governor of Mantua and Reggio, three of his most charming letters, in their comedy, their observation of character, their dramatic quality, their satire, and their suggestion of Florentine life (Nos. 179, 182, 183).

From a fragment of 1524 (No. 186) we learn that the writer is at Sant'Andrea, not from necessity but to secure quiet in which to work on his *History of Florence*. In the city it appears there were too many distractions and interruptions. Machiavelli vaguely alludes to matters connected with the work that he wishes to talk over with his friend, apparently already enough discussed so that Guicciardini would understand. Could it be other than the historian's treatment of the Medici? He decides he will tell the truth diplomatically enough to make complaint impossible.

In August 1525 begins a group of letters to Guicciardini

---

[1] Perhaps the best guide to the meaning of *constable* is Machiavelli's use of the word in his *Art of War*, bk 2, where he is an officer in charge of four hundred men—not, therefore, a man of exalted rank.

covering more than a year, dealing with a variety of subjects, political and personal. We get rare glimpses of Niccolò as author, discussing a proposed staging of his *Mandragola* (Nos. 196, 198, 202). Here are letters on the marriages of Guicciardini's daughters, revealing willingness to make practical exertions for a friend, and skill in delicate personal negotiation (Nos. 196, 199, 200, 211). Recounting his inspection of some farms belonging to Guicciardini, Machiavelli appears as the Tuscan landowner, like his father Bernardo (No. 192). If for Niccolò Sant'-Andrea had been a retreat from the distractions or the summer heat of Florence, the place would have been as pleasant to him as he imagines one of Guicciardini's villas might be to the owner and his guests. Only poverty, with consequent forced winter residence, made his villa unpleasant to Machiavelli. His lively observation for his friend gives the atmosphere of country life, gracious and profitable, though not without trials, in which Bernardo passed his years, as we learn from his *Book of Records*.

In these letters Machiavelli mingles marriage portions for his friend's daughters with the vexed politics of the day: if the Pope realizes his own condition, he will know that Guicciardini's abilities are necessary to him and will wish to please his officer by contributing to his daughter's dower (No. 202). With his unceasing desire for military preparation before the barbarian deluge, he makes what he calls a startling suggestion, already—he says—in the mouths of the common people of Florence, namely that Giovanni de' Medici[2] should be made Florentine general. Lord Giovanni seems to have the qualities of a great soldier: "There is no leader whom the soldiers would more gladly follow, and whom the Spanish more fear and more respect; everybody thinks that Lord Giovanni is bold, prompt, has great

[2] Now known as Giovanni delle Bande Nere—Giovanni of the Black Bands. [His soldiers changed their white ensigns to black on the deaths of Pope Leo X and of their leader.]

ideas, is a maker of great plans" (No. 204). In short, he is a leader who has taken to heart the lessons of Machiavelli's *Art of War*.

Letter no. 222, from Imola, where Machiavelli had gone on army business, is addressed to his son Guido, then a schoolboy. Less than a week later, Guido replied, answering his father's questions and asking for information about the possible coming of the enemy. There is still in the villa much property that should be removed to safety. One may suppose that the twenty or twenty-three barrels of oil he mentions were the produce of the farms, and would account for part of the ninety florins of annual income received from them. In his *Book of Records* Bernardo speaks of selling oil that had to be moved from Sant'Andrea (p. 40, etc.). Guido also tells of studies in music he is about to begin. In grammar he has gone as far as the participles. His master has read to him almost all of the first book of Ovid's *Metamorphoses*; he hopes on his father's return to repeat it to him from memory. We may trust that the recitation was one of Niccolò's pleasures in the two months of life remaining to him after he read this letter.

The Letters

No. 3

9 March 1498, Florence
To Ricciardo Bechi, in Rome

[Savonarola was a Dominican, Prior of St Mark's. As a popular preacher and a moral and political reformer, he attained great influence in Florence, for a time defying Pope Alexander VI. When this letter was written, he was approaching the end of his career. He was executed on 23 May 1498.]

[Savonarola]

In order to give you a full account of affairs here about the Frate, according to your wish, I can tell you that after the two sermons were delivered, of which you have already received copies, he preached on the Sunday of the Carnival, and after saying many things, he invited his followers to receive Communion on the day of the Carnival in San Marco, and said he was going to pray to God that if the things predicted did not come from Him, He would show a clear sign of it. And this he did, as some say, in order to unite his party and make it stronger to defend him, fearing that the Signoria newly chosen, but not announced, would be opposed to him. On the announcement on Monday of the Signoria, of which you must have had full notice, he judged it more than two-thirds hostile to him, and the Pope sent a letter that summoned him, under penalty of interdiction. Hence, being afraid that the Signoria would require him to obey at once, he determined, either on his own notion or advised by others, to give up preaching in Santa Reparata and go to San Marco. Therefore the Thursday morning when the Signoria took office, he said, still in Santa Reparata, that to remove dissension and preserve the honor of God, he was going to draw back,[1] and that men should come to listen to him in San Marco, and women should go to San Lorenzo for Fra Domenico.

Our Frate being, therefore, in his own house, now to hear with what boldness he began his sermons, and with how much he continued them, would have caused you no little wonder. Because, fearing greatly for himself and believing that the new Signoria would not be hesitant about harming him, and having determined that many citizens should be crushed by his fall, he began with great terrors, with reasons that for those who did not examine them were very convincing, showing that his followers were the best of men and his adversaries the most wicked, using every expression he could to weaken the adverse party and strengthen his own. Of these things, because I was present, I shall briefly run through a number.

The text of his first sermon in San Marco was this passage from *Exodus*: "The more they afflicted them, the more they multiplied and grew." And before he came to the explanation of these words, he showed for what reason he had drawn back, and said: "Prudence is straight thinking in practical matters." Then he said that all men have had and now have an end, but diverse. "For Christians, their end is Christ; for other men, both present and past, it has been and is something else, according to their religion. Being directed, then, we who are Christians, to this end which is Christ, we ought with the greatest prudence and observation of the times to preserve his honor; and when the time asks us to risk our lives to risk them for him; and when it is time for a man to conceal himself, to conceal oneself, as we read of Christ and of Saint Paul; and so, he added, we ought to do and we have done.[2] Therefore, when it was time to resist fury, we have done so, as happened on

---

[1] From his defiant position.
[2] *We* means Savonarola himself.

Ascension Day, because so the honor of God and the tin
demanded. Now that the honor of God requires that w̶
yield to wrath, we have yielded."

And having given this short discourse, he indicated two
companies: one which serves under God, namely, himself
and his followers; the other under the Devil, namely, his
opponents. And having spoken of it at length, he entered
upon the exposition of the words of *Exodus* already given,
and said that through tribulations, good men grew in two
ways, in spirit and in number; in spirit, because man unites
himself more closely to God by overcoming adversity, and
becomes stronger as nearer to his active cause, just as hot
water brought close to the fire becomes hotter, because it
is nearer its active cause. They also grow in number, because there are three sorts of men, that is, the good (and
these are the ones who follow him), the perverse and obstinate (and these are his adversaries); and there is a further
kind of men of free lives, given to pleasure, not stubborn in
doing evil nor devoted to doing well, because they see
neither of them clearly. But when between the good and
the perverse there appears some practical difference, "since
opposites when placed near one another stand out more
clearly," they recognize the malice of the wicked and the
simplicity of the good, and draw to the latter and avoid the
former, because naturally everybody avoids evil and follows good gladly; and therefore in adversities the wicked
grow fewer and the good multiply, "and therefore the
more," etc. I present it to you briefly, because the limits of
a letter do not permit a long narrative. He said next—having digressed, as his custom is, further to weaken his
adversaries, and also to make a bridge to his next sermon
—that our discords might cause a tyrant to rise up who
would destroy our houses and lay waste our fields; and
this was not at all opposed to what he had already said,
that Florence was going to prosper and to master Italy,

87

because it will come about that in a short time the tyrant will be driven out. And with this he ended his sermon.

The next morning, again still explaining *Exodus* and coming to that passage where it is said that Moses killed an Egyptian, he said that the Egyptian stood for wicked men, and Moses for the preacher who killed them by revealing their vices, and he said: "O Egyptian! I am going to give you a stab." And then he turned the leaves of your books, O priests, and made such a mess of you that a dog would have turned away from you. Then he added—and that was obviously where he was heading—that he wanted to give the Egyptian another wound and a big one; and he said that God had told him that a man in Florence was trying to make himself tyrant, and was negotiating and using ways for attaining this goal; and that his attempt to drive out the Frate, to excommunicate the Frate, to persecute the Frate, came to nothing else than that he wanted to make himself a tyrant; and that the laws should be kept. And he said so much about it that men later that day publicly guessed about a man who is as near to being a tyrant as you are to Heaven.

But after this, the Signoria having written in his behalf to the Pope, and he himself seeing that he no longer needed to fear his adversaries in Florence, whereas earlier he sought only to unite his party by speaking evil of his adversaries and to frighten them with the name of tyrant, now that he sees he no longer needs to, he has changed his cloak. So, encouraging them to share in the union that has begun, and making no further mention of the tyrant and of their wickedness, he tries to set all of them against the Supreme Pontiff, and, snapping at him, says of him what could be said of the wickedest man you can think of. Thus, according to my judgment, he keeps on working with the times and making his lies plausible.

Now what the masses are saying, what men hope or

88

fear, I leave you to judge, since you are prudent, because you can judge better than I can, since you know all about our factions and the nature of the times, and also, through being in Rome, know the Pontiff's intentions. Only this I beg of you, that if you have not felt that reading this letter of mine is burdensome, you will not find it a burden to tell me in answer what judgment of such a disposition of times and of purposes you make about our affairs. Farewell.

Your Niccolò di M. Bernardo Machiavelli

No. 103

20 November 1509, Verona
To the Honorable Luigi Guicciardini,
as his dearest brother, in Mantua.
Written in the house of G. Borromeo.

[Machiavelli was at this time on a government mission from Florence to the Emperor Maximilian I, then in northern Italy with his army. Luigi Guicciardini was one of a well-known Florentine family, of which Francesco the historian, mentioned in the letter, is the most famous.]

[Personal matters; the difficulties of his mission
to the Emperor]

My dearest Luigi:

Today I have received your letter of the twenty-fifth, which has caused me more concern than if I had lost the lawsuit, since I learned that a little fever has come back to Jacopo. Still your prudence, the assiduity of Marco, the skill of the doctors, the patience and goodness of Jacopo give me confidence that you will drive it away like a filthy whore, an ass, a shameless pig. And from your first letter I expect to learn that in spite of it you have gone off completely happy toward Florence.

I am here in Isola, high and dry like you, because here nothing is known about anything; and yet, in order to seem alive, I keep imagining endless letters that I write to the Ten, and I am sending you their letter unsealed, which, when all of you have read it, you can give it to Giovanni, who will send it by the first courier when Pandolfino writes, or as he thinks best. Give him my regards and tell him that I am here with his Stephen, and am having a good time.

I would have gone to court, but Lang is not there, to whom I have the letter of introduction, and to the Emperor I have no letter, so that I might be arrested as a spy. Then every day it is said he is coming, and all those Mamelukes that follow the court are in control there.

I am glad you have sent those pledges to Florence, for which you deserve great praise from God and from the men of the world.

If you write to your Messer Francesco, tell him that I send my regards to the society. I am yours, very much yours; and as to composing, I reflect on it always. Good bye.

20 November 1509

No. 115

September 1512, Florence
To an unidentified lady.

[This letter describes the restoration of the Medici to Florence by a Spanish army led by the Vicar or Viceroy of King Ferdinand. The Gonfalonier mentioned is Piero Soderini, during whose regime Machiavelli was Secretary of the Second Chancellery in Florence.]

[The return of the Medici to Florence]

Since your Ladyship wishes, Noble Madam, to learn of
the strange events in Tuscany which took place in recent
days, I shall gladly relate them to you, both to please you,
and for the reason that their outcome honored the friends
of Your Illustrious Ladyship and my masters, which two
reasons cancel all the other unpleasant results, which are
countless, as Your Ladyship will understand as I relate
these matters.

It was decided in the meeting at Mantua to put the
Medici back in Florence, and when the Vicar left to return
to Modena, it was much feared in Florence that the Spanish
army would come into Tuscany. Nonetheless, there being
no further assurance of it, on account of their having carried on things secretly in the meeting, and many not being
able to believe that the Pope would want the Spanish army
to upset that province, especially since they knew from
letters from Rome that between the Spanish and the Pope
there was no great confidence, we remained with minds uncertain, without making any preparation, until from
Bologna came assurance of everything. And the hostile
soldiers being already only a day's journey from our bound-
aries, all the city was at once disturbed by this sudden, and
almost unexpected, attack. And having considered what
ought to be done, we decided with all the speed possible,
since we were not in time to guard the passes of the mountains, to send to Firenzuola, a town on the borders between
Florence and Bologna, 2000 infantry, in order that the
Spaniards, so as not to leave behind them so large a force,
would undertake the siege of that town and give us time
to increase the number of our soldiers and resist their attacks with larger forces. At the beginning we thought we
would not put our soldiers in the field, because we did not

judge them powerful enough to resist the enemy, but would assemble them at Prato, a large town lying in the plain at the base of the mountains that come down from the Mugello, ten miles distant from Florence. We judged that place fit to hold our army, which could remain there in security, and because it was near Florence, we could at any time reinforce it if the Spaniards went in that direction.

When this decision was made, all the forces were moved into the places indicated. But the Vicar, whose intention was not to attack the towns but to come to Florence to make a change in the government, hoping with the aid of the Party to do it easily, paid no attention to Firenzuola but, crossing the Apennines, came down to Barberino di Mugello, a town eighteen miles from Florence. All the towns of that region, being completely without garrisons, without resistance received his orders and furnished his army with food according to their ability. Meanwhile a good part of our soldiers were brought to Florence and the leaders of the men-at-arms met and considered defense against this attack. They advised that our soldiers should assemble not at Prato but at Florence, because they judged that if they were shut up in Prato they could not resist the Vicar. Though his forces were not yet known, our generals believed, since he came so boldly into this province, that they were such that their army could not resist them; and therefore they considered withdrawing them to Florence more secure, where with the help of the people they were enough to defend that city, and with this arrangement they could try to hold Prato, leaving there a garrison of three thousand soldiers.

This decision was pleasing, and especially to the Gonfalonier, since he judged himself more secure and stronger against the Party, when he had more forces within the city near himself. And finding things in these conditions, the Vicar sent ambassadors to Florence, who set forth to the

Signoria that they did not come into this province as enemies and did not wish to make any change in the liberty of the city or in its government, but merely wished to make sure that she would leave the French party and join the League, which did not believe it could be sure of that city or of what was promised to it while Piero Soderini was gonfalonier, knowing him as a partisan of the French; and therefore they wished that he would lay aside that rank, and that the people of Florence would choose another more to their liking.

To this the Gonfalonier replied that he had not come to that office with either deceit or force, but that he had been put there by the people; and therefore if all the kings in the world united together should order him to lay it down, never would he lay it down; but if the Florentine people wished him to go, he would do it gladly, just as he gladly took it when, without any ambition of his, the people granted it to him. And in order to test the spirit of the populace, as soon as the ambassador had gone, he assembled all the council and, putting before them the Vicar's proposition, announced that if it pleased the people and if they judged that his departure would bring about peace, then he was ready to go to his house, because he had never thought of anything but benefiting the city, and it would be a grief to him if for love of him she should suffer. This thing with one accord everybody rejected, and he had offers from all to lay down even their lives for his defense.

It happened meanwhile that the Spanish army reached Prato and made a great attack; not taking her, His Excellency negotiated about an agreement with the Florentine ambassador, and sent him to Florence with one of his men, offering to be satisfied with a certain amount of money; and as to the Medici, he would turn over their case to His Catholic Majesty, who might beg, not force, the Florentines to receive them. The ambassadors having arrived with this proposal, reporting the condition of the Spaniards bad, asserting that they would die of hunger and that Prato was going to be held, it put so much confidence into the Gonfalonier and into the multitude by which he was governed that though that peace was advised by the wise, yet the Gonfalonier kept on delaying. The second day afterward news came that Prato was taken, for the Spaniards, having broken part of the wall, pressed back those who defended it and frightened them, so that after not much resistance all fled, and the Spanish, occupying the town, sacked it and killed the people in a miserable scene of distress. To Your Ladyship I shall not repeat the details in order not to cause you any depression of spirits. I shall say merely that more than four thousand were killed and the others were captured and in different ways were forced to ransom themselves; and they did not spare virgins who were cloistered in the holy places, all of which they filled with rape and sacrilege.

This news caused great disturbance in the city. None the less, the Gonfalonier was not frightened, trusting in certain empty opinions. And he was counting on holding Florence and making an agreement with the Spaniards for any sum of money whatever, if only the Medici were kept out. But his board of negotiators having gone, and brought back the answer that it was necessary to receive the Medici or to be ready for war, everybody feared that the city would be sacked, on account of the cowardice of our soldiers in Prato. This fear was increased by all the nobility who wished to change the government, so that Monday evening, the thirtieth of August, at two o'clock at night, our ambassadors received authority to agree with the Vicar no matter what.

And so much did everybody's fear grow that the Palace and the usual protection by the soldiers of the government were given up; and since it was without guards, the Signoria was obliged to release many citizens, who, being considered suspicious and friends of the Medici, had been held under strong guard many days in the Palace. They, along with many others of the most noble citizens of this city, who wished to get back their reputation, took courage. Hence on Tuesday morning they came armed to the Palace, and having seized all the places in order to force the Gonfalonier to leave, were persuaded by some citizens not to use violence but to let him go by agreement. And so the Gonfalonier, accompanied by those same men, returned to his house, and the next night a large company, with the consent of the Signors, took him to Siena.

The magnificent Medici, after hearing what had happened, preferred not to come to Florence, unless first they settled the affairs of the city with the Vicar, with whom after some difficulties they made an agreement; and entering Florence, they were received by all the people with the utmost honor. There was established meanwhile in Florence a certain new order of government, in which it did not seem to the Vicar that there was security for the house of Medici or for the League; therefore he indicated to the Signors of the city that it was necessary to put the government in the form it had during the lifetime of the Magnificent Lorenzo. The noble citizens wished to accede to this, but feared that the multitude would not join in, and while they were carrying on this debate on how they would deal with these things, the Legate entered Florence and with His Lordship came many soldiers and especially Italians. And the Signors of the city brought many citizens together in the Palace on the sixteenth day of the present month—and with them was the Magnificent Giuliano—and while they were talking about reform of the government, they heard a commotion in the Public Square, and Ramazzotto

Medici

with his soldiers and others immediately seized the Palace, shouting: "Palle, palle." [1] And at once the whole city was under arms, and through every part of the city resounded that name, so that the Signors were obliged to summon the people to an assembly, which we call a parliament, where a law was passed by which the magnificent Medici were reinstated in all the honors and ranks of their ancestors. And this city remains very quiet, and hopes not to live less honored with their aid than she lived in times gone by, when the Magnificent Lorenzo their father, of most happy memory, was ruling.

You have, then, Most Illustrious Madam, the detailed account of our affairs, among which I have not cared to include those matters that might distress you, as wretched and little necessary. On the others I have enlarged as much as the narrow limits of a letter permit. If I have satisfied you, I shall be very glad; if not, I pray that Your Most Illustrious Ladyship will excuse me. Long and prosperously may you live.

[Niccolò Machiavelli]

[1] The cry of the supporters of the Medici, derived from the balls in that family's coat of arms.

No. 116

January 1513, Florence
To Piero Soderini, in Ragusa[1]

[Piero Soderini is the Gonfalonier mentioned in the preceding letter, now in Ragusa for safety.]

[1] This letter is apparently a rough draft with notes for expansion and addition. When a clause appears in two forms, I have given but one. The sentences in brackets give such of the notes as may interest the reader.

A letter of yours was given to me in a hood;[2] yet after ten words I recognized it. I believe in the crowds at Piombino to see you, and of your hindrances and Filippo's I am certain, because I know one is harmed by a little light, the other by too much. January does not trouble me, if only February supports me with his hands. I am sorry about Filippo's suspicion, and in suspense wait for its end. [He who does not know how to fence overcomes him who knows.]

Your letter was short and I by rereading it made it long. It was pleasing to me because it gave me a chance to do what I feared to do and what you remind me that I should not do; and this part alone I have observed in it as without application. At this I would wonder, if my fate had not shown me so many and such varied things that I am obliged to wonder but little, or to confess that I have not comprehended while reading and experiencing the actions of men and their methods of procedure.

I understand you and the compass by which you navigate; and if it could be condemned, which it cannot, I would not condemn it, seeing to what port it has taken you and with what hope it can feed you. Consequently, I see, not with your mirror, where nothing is seen but prudence, but with that of the many, which is obliged in affairs to judge the result when they are finished, and not the means while they are going on. Each man according to his own imagination guides himself. And I see various kinds of conduct bringing about the same thing, as by various roads one comes to the same place, and many who work differently attaining the same end—and anything needed to confirm this opinion the actions of this Pontiff and their effects have furnished.

Hannibal and Scipio, besides their military attainments,

---

[2] Disguised, perhaps not in his own hand. Parts, especially of the first paragraph, were probably intended to be unintelligible except to writer and recipient.

in which the two excelled equally, one of them with cruelty, treachery, and lack of religion kept his armies united in Italy and made himself admired by the people, who to follow him rebelled against the Romans; the other achieved the same result in Spain with mercy, loyalty and piety; both of them won countless victories. But because it is not usual to bring up the Romans, Lorenzo de' Medici disarmed the people to hold Florence; Messer Giovanni Bentivogli in order to hold Bologna armed them; the Vitelli in Castello and the present Duke of Urbino in his territory destroyed the fortresses in order to retain those states; Count Francesco and many others built them in their territories to make themselves sure of them. [To test Fortune, who is the friend of young men, and to change according to what you find. But it is not possible to have fortresses and not to have them, to be both cruel and compassionate.] The Emperor Titus believed that he would lose his position on any day when he did not benefit somebody; some others might believe they would lose theirs on the day when they did anybody a favor. To many, weighing and measuring everything, success comes in their undertakings. [As Fortune tires, anything may be ruined. The family, the city, every man has his Fortune founded on his way of proceeding, and each Fortune tires, and when she is tired, she must be got back in another way. Comparison of the horse and the bridle about fortresses.] This Pope Julius, who hasn't a pair of scales or a yardstick in his house, gains through chance—although unarmed— what through organization and arms he scarcely could attain.

We have seen and see every day those I have mentioned and countless others who could be used as instances gaining kingdoms and sovereignties, or falling, according to circumstances; and a man who was praised while he was gaining is reviled when he is losing; and frequently after long prosperity a man who finally loses does not in any way blame himself but accuses the heavens and the action of the Fates. But the reason why different ways of working are sometimes equally effective and equally damaging I do not know, but I should much like to know. So in order to get your opinion I shall be so presumptuous as to give mine.

I believe that as Nature has given men different faces, so she has given them different dispositions and different imaginations. From this it results that each man conducts himself according to his disposition and his imagination. And on the other hand, because times vary and affairs are of varied types, one man's desires come out as he had prayed they would; and that man is fortunate who harmonizes his procedure with his time, but on the contrary he is not fortunate who in his actions is out of harmony with his time and with the type of its affairs. Hence it can well happen that two men working differently come to the same end, because each of them adapts himself to what he encounters, for affairs are of as many types as there are provinces and states. Thus, because times and affairs in general and individually change often, and men do not change their imaginings and their procedures, it happens that a man at one time has good fortune and at another time bad.

And certainly anybody wise enough to understand the times and the types of affairs and to adapt himself to them would have always good fortune, or he would protect himself always from bad, and it would come to be true that the wise man would rule the stars and the Fates. But because there never are such wise men, since men in the first place are short-sighted, and in the second cannot command their natures, it follows that Fortune varies and commands men, and holds them under her yoke. And to verify this opinion, I think the instances given above, on which I have based it, are enough, and so I expect one to support the other.

Cruelty, treachery and irreligion are enough to give reputation to a new ruler in a province where humanity, loyalty and religion have been common practice for a long time, while humanity, loyalty and religion are sufficient where cruelty, treachery and irreligion have dominated for a time, because, as bitter things disturb the taste and sweet ones cloy it, so men get bored with good and complain of ill. These causes, among others, opened Italy to Hannibal and Spain to Scipio, and so both of them found times and things suited to their way of proceeding. At that very time a man like Scipio would not have been so successful in Italy, or one like Hannibal so successful in Spain, as they both were in the provinces wherein they acted.

Niccolò Machiavelli

No. 117

13 March 1513, Florence
To the Magnificent Francesco Vettori, most Worthy Florentine Ambassador to the Supreme Pontiff at Rome.

[Vettori was ambassador to Pope Julius II, appointed by the Medici government now powerful in Florence. The Lord of the last paragraph is Cardinal Giovanni de'Medici, soon to be Pope Leo X.]

[Longing for employment by the Medici]

Magnificent Sir: As you have learned from Pagolo Vettori, I have got out of prison amid the universal rejoicing of this city, even though I hoped for it because of your doings and those of Pagolo, for which I thank you. I won't go over again the long story of my misfortune, but will merely say that Luck has done everything to cause me this trouble. Yet, thanks be to God! it is over. I hope I won't run into it again, both because I shall be more careful and because the times will be more liberal and not so suspicious.

You know in what condition I found our friend Messer Totto. I ask favor for him from you and Pagolo generally. He wants only, he and I, this special thing, that he may be put among the servants of the Pope, and written in his record, and have the patent for it. For these things we beg you.

Keep me, if it is possible, in our Lord's memory, so that, if it is possible, he or his family may employ me in something or other, because I believe I would bring honor to him and profit to myself.

13 March 1512   Your Niccolò Machiavelli
in Florence

No. 119

18 March 1513, Florence
To the Magnificent Francesco Vettori, Florentine Ambassador to the Supreme Pontiff at Rome.

[See the preceding letter. The Magnificent Giuliano is Giuliano de'Medici, Duke of Nemours, immortalized by Michelangelo's statue on his tomb in San Lorenzo, Florence. Machiavelli thanks him for bringing about his release after his arrest on suspicion—unwarranted—of conspiracy against the Medici. Giovanni de'Medici was chosen Pope on 11 March.]

[Bad Fortune resisted]

Magnificent Ambassador:

Your very friendly letter has made me forget all my past troubles, and though I was more than certain of your love for me, this letter has been most pleasing to me. I thank you as much as I can and pray to God that to your profit and benefit he will give me power to do something that will please you, because I can say that all of life that is left me I consider I owe to the Magnificent Giuliano and your Pagolo.

And as to turning my face to resist Fortune, I want you to get this pleasure from my distresses, namely, that I have borne them so bravely that I love myself for it and feel that I am stronger than you believed. And if these masters of mine decide not to let me lie on the ground, I shall be glad of it, and believe I shall conduct myself in such a way that they too will have reason to approve. If they decide differently, I'll get on as when I came here, for I was born poor and I learned earlier to stint myself than to prosper. And if you remain there, I'll come to pass some time with you, when you advise me to. And, not to be more tedious, I send my regards to you and to Pagolo, to whom I am not writing, because I don't know what further to say to him.

I related the chapter about Filippo to some of our friends, who rejoiced that he had got there safely. They were very sorry about the small esteem and value that Giovanni Cavalcanti has for him; and when trying to discover the reason for this state of things, they discovered that little Brancaccio[1] told Messer Giovanni that Filippo had been instructed by his brother to recommend Giovanni, Ser Antonio's son, to the Pope, and for that reason Messer Giovanni was unwilling to admit him; and they greatly blame Giuliano because he should have quieted this scandal, even though it was not true; and if it was true, they blame Filippo for taking certain desperate remedies, so advise him to be more cautious next time.

[1] Brancaccio, often mentioned in the letters to Vettori, seems otherwise unknown.

And tell Filippo that Niccolò degli Agli trumpets it throughout Florence, and I do not know the reason, but without scruple and without excusing anything, he blames him in such a way that there isn't a man who doesn't wonder at it. So suggest to Filippo that if he knows the cause of this enmity, he provide against it in some way; and just yesterday he came to see me with a list in his hand giving all the gossips in Florence, and he told me that he went recruiting those who would speak ill of Filippo, to get revenge on him. I wish to let you know, so you can mention it to him, and I send him my regards.

The whole group sends regards to you, beginning with Tommaso del Bene and going as far as our Donato. And every day we are in the house of some girls to recover our strength; and only yesterday we were in the house of Sandra di Pero to see the processions pass; and so we go spending our time on these general rejoicings, getting pleasure from what is left of life, so that I feel as though I were dreaming.

Farewell. Florence, 18 March 1512.

Niccolò Machiavelli

No. 120

April 9, 1513, Florence
To Francesco Vettori, in Rome.

[I must discuss public affairs or be silent]

Magnificent Mr. Ambassador:

And I, who of his color had become aware, said: "How shall I go if you are fearful, who in my timidity are always my encouragement?"[1]

---

[1] Dante, *Inferno* 4.16-18.

This letter of yours has terrified me more than the rack, and I grieve over any notion you have that I am angry, not on my own account, because I am trained no longer to wish for anything with passion, but on yours. I beg you to imitate the others, who with persistence and craft, rather than with ability and prudence, make themselves places. And as to that story about Totto, it displeases me if it displeases you. Otherwise I am not bothering about it, and if we can't roll it, let's bowl it along.[2] Once and for all let me tell you that you are not to take any trouble about the things I ask of you, because if I don't have them I shall not get excited about them.

If you are sick of discussing affairs, as the result of many times seeing things turn out contrary to the notions and concepts you form, you are right, because the like has happened to me. Yet if I could speak to you, I couldn't keep from filling your head with castles in Spain, because Fortune has determined that since I don't know how to talk about the silk business or the wool business, or about profits and losses, I have to talk about the government, and I must either make a vow of silence or discuss that.

If I could get outside our territory, I should surely go, I too, to see if the Pope is at home; but among so many favors, mine through my neglect was forgotten. I shall wait for September. I learn that Cardinal Soderini has a great deal of business with the Pope. I wish you would advise me if you think it wise for me to write him a letter asking that he recommend me to His Holiness; or if it would be better that by word of mouth you attend to this affair on my behalf with the Cardinal; or if nothing should be done—on which perhaps you will give me a word in reply.

As to the horse, you make me laugh by reminding me about it; because you are to pay me when I remember it and not otherwise.

2 Apparently proverbial.

Our archbishop by this hour must be dead, and may God receive his soul and those of all his family. Farewell.

Niccolò Machiavelli, formerly Secretary

No. 122

16 April 1513, Florence
To Francesco Vettori . . . His Patron and Benefactor.

[The Pope under whom Machiavelli wishes employment is Pope Leo X, Giovanni de'Medici.]

[Florentine comedy; desire for employment]

Magnificent · Ambassador:

Last Saturday I wrote to you, and though I haven't anything to say or to write, I don't want this Saturday to pass by without my writing.

The company that you know all about seems as though it were lost, because there isn't a dovecot that will hold us, and all its leaders have been boiling. Tommaso has become queer, difficult, fussy, stingy to such an extent that when you return he will seem to you another man. And I want to tell you what has happened to me.

Last week he bought seven pounds of veal and sent it to Marione's house. Then he thought he had spent too much and wanted to find somebody who would share the cost, so he went hunting for somebody who would have dinner with him. Moved by pity, I went, with two others, whom I hunted up for him. We had dinner, and when we came to figure the expense it amounted to fourteen soldi each. I had only ten with me; so I owed him four soldi; and every day he asks me for them; and just yesterday evening he dunned me on the Ponte Vecchio. You may not think he's wrong about that; but it is nothing to the other things he does.

Girolamo del Guanto's wife died, and for three or four days he was like a dazed barbel.[1] Then he came to life and wanted to get another wife, and every evening we have been on the bench of the Capponi discussing this marriage. Count Orlando is all torn up again over a fellow from Ragusa and is not able to get any kindness from him. Donato del Corno has opened another shop where doves are sold, and he goes all day from the old to the new one and is like a crazy man, and now he goes off with Vincenzio, now with Pizzo, now with one of his boys, now with another; yet I have never seen that he is angry with Riccio. I don't know the cause of this; some think anything would be more to his purpose than the lot; I for my part can't make any sense out of it. Filippo di Bastiano has returned to Florence, and complains terribly of Brancaccino, but in general, and as yet has not come to any details. If he goes to Rome, I shall let you know, so you can warn him.

So then if sometimes I laugh or sing, I do it because I have just this one way for expressing my anxious sorrow.[2]

If it is true that Jacopo Salviati and Matteo Strozzi have been let go, you will continue there as the public agent; and since Jacopo does not stay there, of those who are coming I see nobody who can stay there so you can be sent away; hence I suppose that you will stay as long as you wish to. His Magnificence Giuliano will come there, and you will naturally find a chance to do me good, and the same thing for the Cardinal of Volterra.[3] So I cannot believe that if my affair is handled with some skill, I won't succeed in being employed at something, if not in behalf of

---

[1] Proverbial. Cf. Pulci, *Morgante*, 20.48.

[2] Petrarch, *Cesare, poi che*. Machiavelli substitutes *expressing* for the *concealing* of the original.

[3] Cardinal Soderini, brother of Piero Soderini, ex-Gonfalonier of Florence.

Florence, at least in behalf of Rome and the Papacy, i
respect to which I ought to be less suspected. And since _
know you are firmly placed there, and you think I cannot
make a move in any other way, and I may run into preju-
dices here, I ought to go there, and I cannot believe that,
if the Serenity of our Lord would employ me, I should not
do myself good and bring profit and honor to all my friends.
I don't write this to you because I want things too much,
nor because I want you to undertake for my love any
burden or trouble or expense or anxiety about anything, but
in order that you may know my intention, and if you can
help me, you may know that what benefits me always benefits you and your family, to which I owe all that is left me.

16 April 1513
Niccolò Machiavelli in Florence.

No. 128

(out of numerical order to fit chronology)
29 April 1513, Florence
To Francesco Vettori, in Rome[1]

[Julius II had recently died and Leo X (Giovanni de'Medici) had become Pope. Henry VIII of England, Maximilian I (Emperor of Germany), and Ferdinand V (King
of Spain) were allied against Louis XII of France and
the Venetians. In the preceding year, the Spanish and
Papal forces had been defeated by the French at Ravenna.
The French, however, partly because of the Swiss hostility,
withdrew from Italy, though still claiming the Dukedom
of Milan. Ferdinand controlled southern Italy.]

[1] The text of this letter exists in more than one form; the differences
are not vital. Alvisi places it after Vettori's letter of 12 July.

[Ferdinand V of Spain, the Catholic; the new prince]

Magnificent Ambassador, Whom I Greatly Honor:

In the midst of my greatest good fortunes I never had anything that pleased me as much as your discussions, because from them I always learned something. Imagine, then, when I find myself now far from any other pleasure, how much I was pleased by your letter, to which nothing was wanting except your presence and the sound of your living voice; and as I have been reading it, for I have read it many times, I always have forgotten my unhappy situation, and I seem to have gone back in memory to my former affairs in which I have uselessly endured so many exertions and spent so much time. And even though I have vowed not to think any more on affairs of state nor to talk about them, as is proved by my coming to my farm and avoiding conversation, nevertheless, to answer your questions, I am forced to break every vow, because I believe I am more obligated to the long-standing friendship I have with you than to any other obligation I have to any person; especially when you do me so much honor as you do at the end of your letter, for, to tell you the truth, I have taken a little pride in it, since it is true "that it is not a small thing to be praised by a praised man." [2] I fear, though, that my notions may seem to you not to have their old flavor, for which I hope it will excuse me that I have deliberately given up such dealings altogether, and besides, that I have learned no details about what is now going on. And you know how well things can be judged in the dark, and especially these. So what I say to you will be based on either the foundation of your discourse or on my presuppositions, as to which, if they are false, I hope you will excuse me for the reason given above.

[2] Cicero, *Familiar Letters* 5.12.7; 15.6.1.

You would like to know, according to your letter of the 21st, what I believe has moved Spain to make this truce with France, since you cannot see anything in it for him, when everything is carefully gone over from all directions; so that on one side judging that the King is wise, and on the other being of the opinion that he has made a mistake, you are forced to believe that it hides some great thing which now neither you nor anybody understands. And truly your discourse could not be more careful or more prudent, nor do I believe that on this matter anything else could be said. Yet to act alive and to obey you, I shall say what occurs to me.

Nothing, I think, makes you hesitate more than the presupposition you lay down of the King of Spain's prudence. I answer that I have always thought Spain[3] more crafty and fortunate than wise and prudent. I do not intend to go over his affairs at length, but will deal with this expedition against France in Italy, made before England could move or Spain could be sure that he was going to move. I earlier thought and still think that in that expedition, notwithstanding its contrary end, without necessity he put into danger all his territories—which is a very rash thing in a prince. I say *without necessity*, because he had seen through signs of the year before, after so much harm that the Pope had done France (attacking his friends, and trying to make Genoa rebel) and also after many provocations that he himself had given to France (by sending his soldiers with those of the Church to injure France's tributaries) that nevertheless France, when victorious (having driven away the Pope and deprived him of all his armies) and able to drive him from Rome and Spain from Naples, did not wish to do so, but turned his mind to a treaty. So Spain could not fear France. Nor is there wisdom in the

[3] The King of Spain, as often in the *Letters*. Similarly the King of England is England, and the King of France is France.

reason brought forward for him, that he did it to make himself sure of the Kingdom,[4] since France had not turned his purpose there, because he was tired out and beset with doubts. And if Spain should say that France did not come ahead then because he had such and such a reason for hesitating, which another time he would not have had, I answer that all those reasons for hesitation that France then had he was going to have always, because always the Pope was going to try to keep Naples from going back to France, and always France was going to be careful about the Pope and the other powers, lest they should unite, on seeing him ambitious.

And if some one says that Spain feared that if he did not unite with the Pope to make war on France, the Pope in anger would unite with France in order to carry on this war against him, since the Pope was a man so violent and full of the devil, and therefore was obliged to make such a decision, I should answer that France always would have made a treaty with Spain sooner than with the Pope, if in those times he had been able to agree with either of them, both because the victory was more certain and France would not have had to use arms, and because then he believed himself greatly injured by the Pope and not by Spain. And to be revenged for that injury and to satisfy the Church with the Council, he always could be either mediator of a solid peace, or composer of a treaty secure for himself. Nevertheless he left behind all those plans and chose war, though he needed to fear that in war with one battle all his states would go, as he feared when he lost the day at Ravenna, for immediately after the news of that defeat he arranged to send Gonsalvo to Naples, for that kingdom was as though lost and the kingdom of Castile was tottering under him. And he had no reason to believe that the Swiss would avenge him and

[4] The kingdom of Naples, for Italy *the* Kingdom.

make him safe, and restore to him his lost reputation, as came about.

So if you will consider that whole action and the handling of those things, you will see in the King of Spain craft and good fortune rather than wisdom or prudence. And when I see a man making a mistake, I suppose he will make a thousand of them; and I do not believe that under this decision he has now made there is anything else than what is seen, because I don't drink the label on a bottle,[5] and in these matters I do not intend that any authority should move me without reason. Hence I hold to the conclusion that Spain may have made a mistake and understood badly and concluded worse.

But let us abandon my opinion and consider him prudent, and let us discuss this decision as that of a wise man. I say, then, making such a presupposition, that in trying properly to find the truth of this matter, I should need to know whether this truce was made after the news of the Pontiff's death and the installation of the new one, or before, because perhaps it would make some difference. But since I do not know, I shall assume it made before the Pope's death. If then—I ask you what you think Spain should have done, being in the condition he is, you would answer what you have written to me, namely, that he could have made peace with France, restoring Lombardy, in order to put him under obligation and to remove all reason for bringing French armies into Italy.

To this I answer that to discuss this affair properly one must note that Spain made that expedition against France with the hope of defeating him, relying perhaps on the Pope, on England, and on the Emperor as foundations more than he should have done, as he learned when finally the test came, because he expected to get money enough

[5] Literally, I do not drink districts, that is, I am not so impressed by the name of the region where a wine is produced that I forget to observe its quality.

from the Pope; and he believed that the Emperor would make a vigorous attack on Burgundy and that England, being young and wealthy and correspondingly eager for glory, would be certain to come in great force whenever he embarked; altogether, then, France would be compelled, both in Italy and at home, to accept his conditions.

Of these things, none came about, because from the Pope he got money only at first and sparingly; but later the Pope not merely did not give him money but every day sought to ruin him and carried on negotiations against him. From the Emperor came nothing further than the journey of the Bishop of Gurk, and slanders and reproaches. From England came a weak force, which could not be combined with his own. Hence, if it had not been for the seizure of Navarre, before France was in the field, both of those armies would have been disgraced, for they would have gained nothing but shame, because one never got out of the forests of Fonterabbia, the other retreated into Pampalona and with difficulty defended it. Hence Spain was exhausted in the midst of this confusion of friends, from whom he could expect nothing better in the future, but rather something worse, because every day they negotiated for an agreement with France. As a result, seeing on the other side France bearing the expense, in agreement with the Venetians, and hoping in the Swiss, he decided that it would be better to be beforehand with the King in whatever way he could, rather than to remain in such great uncertainty and confusion, and under unbearable expense; because I have heard from a good source that a man who is in Spain writes that there is no money and no way of getting it, and that his army is only of conscripts, who moreover are not obeying him.

So I believe his plan has been, in this truce, to make his allies realize their mistake and make them more forward in the war, as a result of his promising the ratification, etc.; or to get the war away from his own country and away from such great expense and danger (if in the spring Pampalona had been captured, he would without doubt have lost Castile, and it is not reasonable that he should wish any longer to run this risk).

As to affairs in Italy, Spain may perhaps be relying more than is reasonable on his own soldiers; but I do not at all believe that he is putting reliance on the Swiss, or on the Pope, or on the Emperor, more than is necessary; and I believe he sees that in this affair eating may lead to drinking by the Emperor and the Italians.[6] And he should not have made a stricter agreement with France, to give him the Dukedom,[7] as you say he should have done, since he had not found France on his side, and also since he should not have judged it a correct decision. Indeed I believe France perhaps would not have made such a treaty, because already he must have made an agreement with the Venetians, and then as a result of not trusting in Spain or in his armies, France would have believed that Spain did not do it for the sake of an agreement with himself, but to ruin France's agreements with others.

As to Spain, I do not see any profit in it for him, because France would become in every way powerful in Italy, however he entered the Dukedom. And if to gain it Spanish arms were enough, to hold it he would need to send his own there, and in large numbers, which could rouse the same suspicions in the Italians and in Spain that would be roused by armies coming to gain it by force. And of loyalty and of promises no one today makes any account. Hence Spain would not see in such conduct any security on one side, and on the other side would see this loss, because he would make this peace with France either with the consent of the allies or not. With their

[6] Necessity and opportunity may teach them to make heavier demands.
[7] Of Milan.

consent, he would judge it impossible, through not being able to bring to agreement Pope and France and Venetians and Emperor, so that to wish to do it by agreement with his allies would be a dream. Needing, then, to do it against their will, he would see in it an evident loss for himself, because he would be joined with a king—and making him powerful—who, every time he had opportunity for it, presumably would remember better old injuries than new benefits, and Spain would have excited against him all the powerful Italians, and those outside Italy, because, since he was the sole rouser of all of them against France, to leave them now would be too great an injury. And therefore, as a result of this peace made as you would like to have had it made, he would have seen the greatness of the King of France sure, the anger of the allies against himself sure, and the loyalty of France uncertain; on the latter alone he must of necessity rely, because having made him powerful and the others angry, he would have to stand with France. But wise princes never put themselves, except through necessity, into the power of another man.

So I conclude that he has judged it a more secure plan to make a truce, because with this truce he shows his allies their mistake, and behaves himself in the meantime, and gives them time to undo it if it does not please them; he gets the war away from home, and again brings into dispute and confusion the affairs of Italy, where he sees that there is matter to undo even yet, and a bone to gnaw. And as I said above, he hopes that eating will teach everybody to drink; and he believes that the Pope, the Emperor, and the Swiss will take no pleasure in the greatness of the Venetians and France in Italy, and judges that if they are not enough to keep France from taking Lombardy, they will at least be enough with his help to keep France from going farther. For this reason Spain supposes that the Pope will have to throw himself entirely into his arms; because he can expect that the Pope will not unite with the Venetians or with their adherents, as the result of the affairs of Romagna. And so with this truce he sees the victory of France uncertain, and that he does not have to trust France, and does not have to fear changes by the confederates. Because the Emperor and England will ratify it or not; if they ratify it, they will consider that this truce is going to aid all and not hurt them; if they do not ratify, they will become more eager for war, and with greater forces and better arranged than in the past year will come to attack France. And in every one of these cases Spain gains his purpose.

I believe, therefore, that his purpose has been this, and that he believes by means of this truce either to force the Emperor and England to make war in earnest, or by means of their reputation, with other ways than arms, to settle things to his advantage. And in every other procedure he would see danger, that is, either in continuing war or making peace against their will; and therefore he took a middle way, from which could come either war or peace.

If you have examined the plans and the advances of this king, you will be less astonished by this truce. This king from a slight and weak position has come to his present greatness, and has had always to struggle with new states and doubtful subjects. And one of the ways with which new states are held and doubtful minds are either made firm or are kept uncertain and unresolved, is to rouse about oneself great expectations, all the time keeping men's minds occupied in considering what is going to be the end of new decisions and new undertakings. Such a necessity this king has recognized and used well. It produced his war in Granada, his attacks on Africa, his entrance into the Kingdom, and all his other well-known and varied enterprises. He saw the end of none of these; indeed his end is not a particular gain or a particular victory, but to give himself reputation among his people and to keep them uncertain among the great number of his affairs. And therefore he is a spirited maker of beginnings, to which he later gives the particular end that is placed before him by chance and that necessity teaches him, and up to now he has not been able to complain of his luck or of his courage. I prove to you this opinion of mine by the division he made with France of the kingdom of Naples, about which he must have been sure that war would have to come of it between him and France, without seeing the end of it by a thousand miles; he could not have believed that he was going to defeat France in Apulia, in Calabria, and at the Garigliano. But it has been enough for him to begin, in order to give himself the reputation he sought, hoping either with Fortune or with trickery to go ahead. And what he has done always, he will still do, and the end of all these plays will show you that such is the truth.

All the preceding things I have said assuming that Pope Julius was alive; but if King Ferdinand had learned of his death and the election of the present Pope, he would have done the same, because if he could not confide in Julius as being unstable, hasty, rash, and stingy, in this one he cannot confide as being wise. And if Spain has any prudence at all, he is not going to be moved by any benefit that was conferred on him in smaller matters, nor any connection they have had, because then he obeyed, now he commands; then he gambled with other men's property, now with his own; then he could profit from confusion, now from peace. And Spain must believe that His Holiness Our Lord will not use either his money or his armies against Christians unless he is coerced; and I believe everybody will hesitate to force him.

I realize that this letter must appear to you a *pastinacca* fish,[8] not of the flavor you expected. My excuse is that my mind is estranged from all these matters, as is shown by my going to my farm, far from every human face. Not knowing what is going on, I am forced to discuss in the dark, and have based everything on the information you have given me. Therefore I pray you to hold me excused. Give my regards to everybody there, especially to your Paolo, if he hasn't left.

Florence, 29 April 1513   Your friend [9]

                                                        N. M.

No. 124

20 June 1513, Florence
To . . . Francesco Vettori.

[See the head-note of the preceding letter.]

[France, England, Spain, the Swiss, and the Pope]

Magnificent Ambassador:

I wrote some weeks ago in reply to a discussion of yours about the truce made between France and Spain. Since then I have had no letters from you, nor have I written, because, understanding that you were about to come home, I waited to speak to you directly. But since I now understand that your return has been put off and that you perhaps are going to stay there some days, I have decided to pay you a visit with this letter and to talk with you about all those things we would talk about if you were here. And though I can only talk wildly, because I am far away from secrets and from events, all the same I do not believe my opinions on affairs can do any harm,

---

[8] Having neither head nor tail.
[9] Apparently this letter was written when Machiavelli was briefly in Florence; within it he speaks of living at his farm.

either to me, when I tell them to you, or to you, when you hear them from me.

You have seen the success up to now of the French campaign in Italy, which has been for the most part contrary to all that could be believed or feared; and this outcome can be counted along with the other pieces of great good fortune that His Holiness the Pope and that splendid Family[1] have had. And because I believe that it is at all times the duty of a prudent man to reflect on what may harm him, and to foresee things when they are at a distance, and to assist what is good and to resist evil in time, I have put myself in the place of the Pope and have examined carefully what I should have to fear now, and what means I should use against them. This I shall write out for you, relying on what has been said by those who can do it better than I can, because of understanding these affairs more exactly.

If I were the Pontiff, I should continue to rely wholly on Fortune, until an agreement was made for laying down arms either entirely or for the most part. And I should not feel sure of the Spaniards if they could be less cautious in Italy than now; and not sure of the Swiss, if they could be less cautious about France and Spain; and not sure of any other who might be the chief power in Italy. So, on the other hand, I should not fear France[2] if he remained on the other side of the mountains or if he returned to Lombardy on an agreement with me. And considering where things are at present, I should be as much afraid of a new agreement as of a new war.

As to the war that might make me return to those suspicions that I felt a few days ago, there is now no other fear except that France may win a great victory over the

[1] Apparently the Medici.
[2] In this letter, as in many other places, "France," "Spain," etc., sometimes mean "the king of France," "the king of Spain," etc., and sometimes just the countries.

English. As to the agreement, it will take place when France makes an agreement with England or with Spain without me. And when I consider whether agreement with England will be easy or not, and also one with Spain, I decide that if one with England is difficult, this with Spain is possible and reasonable; and if we don't keep an eye on it, I greatly fear that it may come unexpectedly upon us, as did the truce between them.

The reasons that influence me are these. I have always believed and now believe that it would please and now pleases Spain to see the King of France out of Italy, provided that with his own arms and his own reputation he drove him out. I have never believed and do not believe that the victory the Swiss won last year over France was altogether pleasing to him. This opinion of mine is based on what is reasonable, since the Pope and the Swiss are too powerful in Italy, and on some reports from which I have learned that Spain complains also of the Pope, since he thinks the latter has given the Swiss too much power, and among the reasons that made him make a truce with France I believe this was one. Now if this first victory displeases Spain, this second that the Swiss have won will,[3] I believe, please him less, because he sees that he is alone in Italy, he sees that the Swiss have a high reputation there, he sees a Pope there who is young, rich and justly eager for glory; the Pope does not wish to make a smaller display of himself than his predecessors have made, and he has brothers and nephews without territory. Spain therefore has good reason to fear him, for if he joins with the Swiss, Spain's possessions may be taken away; and there is little that Spain can do if the Pope decides to do it. And Spain cannot provide against it more securely than by making an agreement with France, by which he could easily gain Navarre, and give France a state difficult

[3] Novara, June 6, 1513.

to retain because of the nearness of the Swiss; and he could deprive the Swiss of their opening for easy passage into Italy, and could make the Pope's use of them less convenient. Such an agreement, when France is in his present situation, the Pope properly would not refuse but actually seek for.

So if I were the Pope and judged this likely to happen, I should try either to disturb it or to be leader in it; and I suspect that conditions may be such that a treaty can easily be concluded between France and Spain, the Pope and the Venetians. I do not put in it the Swiss or the Emperor or England, because I judge that England is going to let himself be ruled by Spain, and I do not see how the Emperor can be in agreement with the Venetians, or how France can come to terms with the Swiss; therefore I let them go and take those from whom the agreement is more to be hoped for; and it seems to me that such an agreement would be enough for all four of them; because it ought to be enough for the Venetians to enjoy Verona, Vicenza, Padua, and Treviso; for the King of France, Lombardy; for the Pope, his own territories; for Spain, the Kingdom. And to bring this about would cause injury merely to a counterfeit Duke of Milan, to the Swiss, and to the Emperor, all of whom would be left ready to attack France. To protect himself from them he would have always to keep his corselet on; and this would make all the others safe from him, and the others would watch one another. Hence in this agreement I see great security and ease, because among them would be a common fear of the Germans that would be the glue to keep them stuck together, and there would not be among them any causes for complaint, except for the Venetians, who would be patient.

Taking it in any other way, I do not see any security,

because I am of the opinion—and I don't believe I an
deceiving myself—that when the king of France is dead
[the next king] will think about a campaign in Lombardy,
and this will always be a reason for keeping his sword
drawn. Otherwise I believe that in any case Spain will
strike a blow at the others; and if the first victory of the
Swiss made him make a truce, this second one will make
him make peace; and I do not value negotiations he carries
on, things that he says, or promises he makes. Such a
peace, if it should be made, would be very dangerous,
if made without the participation of the others.

Farewell.

Florence, 20 June 1513
Niccolò Machiavelli.

No. 125

26 June 1513, Florence
To Master Giovanni di Francesco Vernacci[1] in Pera.

[Niccolò's misfortunes; God's help; business]

Dearest Giovanni:

I have received several of your letters, and finally
one of last April, in which and in the others you complain that you have not received mine. I answer that
after your departure I had so many worries that it is no
wonder I didn't write; it is rather a miracle that I am
alive, because my office has been taken from me and I
have been on the point of losing my life, which God
and my innocence have saved for me. I have endured
all sorts of evils, both of prison and other things. Yet by

[1] A sister's son.

the grace of God I am well, and I manage to live as I can and so I'll try to do, until the heavens show themselves more favorable.[2]

You have written to me several times that I should see about lightening the taxes on your farm. On this I say that it is necessary for you to be here, and you will not be too late for the things that have to be done, because you will always be early enough.

Marietta and all of us are well; try to keep well so that you can prosper in something.

Lorenzo Machiavelli complains about you and says that you do not explain clearly, because, as to one-half of the cloth that remains in your possession, you say that you have sold it for future payment and trusted it to I don't know whom, and you do not tell him the price, and the man to whom you say you have trusted it asserts that you are not correct. So I beg that you will write things out clearly and will go to the extreme of writing too much rather than too little, so that he can't rightfully complain about you.

Greet the consul on my behalf and tell him that I had his letter, and that I am alive and well, and have nothing else that is good. Christ keep you.

Niccolò Machiavelli in Florence.

26 June 1513.

No. 129

4 August 1513, Florence
To Master Giovanni di Francesco Vernacci, in the Levant.

[2] The remainder of this letter is printed in Lesca's edition, Florence 1929.

[Florentine commerce in the Levant]

Dearest Giovanni:

I wrote you about a month ago and told you what was happening to me and especially the reasons why I hadn't written to you before. I assume you got it, so I shall not repeat further. I received your letter of 26 May, to which it does not occur to me to say other than that we are all well; and Marietta had a baby girl that died after three days; Marietta is well.

I wrote to you before that Lorenzo Machiavelli did not feel satisfied with you, and especially with your reports, because he said you reported to him seldom and after delay, so that he did not get from your letters anything sure. I advise you therefore to write to those with whom you do business so clearly that when they have a letter of yours they may think they are there—in such detail it describes the thing to them. And as to sending you anything more, he has said to me that if he does not finish this piece of business entirely and come out clear, he intends not to undertake any other.

A certain Neri del Benino, brother-in-law of Giovanni Machiavelli, has come here, to whom Giovanni has given cloth; and therefore it is not proper that he should deal with anybody else. And Filippo wishes to sell it at the fair.

Try to keep healthy and attend to business, because I know that if you keep healthy and do your duty, you will not lack anything. I am well in body but in everything else ill. I have no other hope but that God will help me, and up to now he has indeed not abandoned me.

Remember me to the consul Juliano Lapi a thousand

times, and tell him I am alive. I have nothing more to say. Christ watch over you.

4 August 1513
Niccolò Machiavelli in Florence.

No. 131

10 August 1513, Sant'Andrea in Percussina[1]
To Francesco Vettori

[See the head-note of Letter of 29 April 1513.]

[Foreign powers in Italy; danger from the Swiss]

Mr. Ambassador:

You do not want this poor King of France to have Lombardy again, and I do want it. I fear that your not wanting and my wanting have the same foundation of a natural affection or passion, which makes you say *No* and me *Yes*. You dignify your *No* by showing that there would be more difficulty in bringing about peace if the King were to return to Lombardy; I have shown, in order to dignify my *Yes*, that such is not the truth, and further that peace made in the method I indicate will be more secure and more solid.

And coming again to particulars, to answer your letter of the fifth, I say I am with you that, as to England, it must always seem strange that he came into France with such great preparation and had to retire; it must be, then, that this retirement is founded on some necessity. I should

---

[1] At this village, about six miles south of Florence, can still be seen the house and farmland which Machiavelli inherited from his father. Their town house in Florence was on Via Guicciardini. After his loss of his secretaryship in 1512, he spent a good deal of time at Sant'Andrea, yet his letters are generally indicated as written in Florence. Florentine custom would have made the country house a usual summer residence.

judge that a necessity great enough would be that to which Spain and the Pope could force him, and I have been judging and now judge that if England should on one side find the attempt difficult, and on the other should see the will of those two, it would be easy to influence him. And if he should be discontented, it would seem to me pertinent, because the more the King of France is or will be weak, so long as he is between the hostile and dreaded English and Swiss, he cannot suppose that he can take other men's property; on the contrary, he will need to suppose that somebody else must protect his own for him. In that case the King of Spain will find his intention carried out, because I believe that in addition to making himself secure in his own states, he has been dreaming that with his armies he could continue as the cock of Italy. And in this situation they will all remain, because France, since he fears England and the Germans are hostile, cannot send a large army into Lombardy. He must therefore depend on Spanish armies in any case.

I do not see that the Swiss by themselves are in a position to make the English yield, because I do not believe they can or will serve France except as hired soldiers. Because they are poor and do not border on England, France must pay them and at a high rate; moreover, he can hire Lanzknechts[2] and get the same service from them, and England would need to fear them quite as much. And if you say that England can get the Swiss to attack France in Burgundy, I answer that this method injures France, and if England is going to yield, France must find a way to injure England. I think Spain and the Pope will not now take up arms against France, but that on one side they will abandon him and on the other side will pretend that their reason for making war on France was

---

[2] German mercenary infantrymen able to render much the same service as the Swiss soldiers.

consideration for the Church, and now that the King has desisted from harming her, they are not going to harm him. So I fully believe that without any stronger medicine England is going to retire, especially since, as I have said many times, he has found and is finding the expedition against France dangerous. And England has to keep in mind that if he comes to a battle and loses it, it could be that thus he would lose his own kingdom as well as France. And if you say to me that he will send money in large amounts to the Germans, and will get France attacked from another side, I answer this with the opinion I have always held, that he will wish, both through pride and through glory, to spend his money on his own people; and besides, anything he sent to the Emperor would be thrown away, and the Swiss would want too much.

I believe also that confidence between Spain and France can develop easily, because it is not to Spain's advantage to destroy the King in this way; and France has seen a test of it, for in the midst of his greatest dangers Spain has suspended arms. And so much the more France will trust in him, as on his side he sees that he is restored in Lombardy, for new benefits are wont to make men forget old injuries. On the other hand, Spain would not need to fear an old king,[3] worn out, and sickly, placed between the English and the Germans, the one suspected and the other hostile; and he would not need to have the Pope's authority defend him, because it would be enough to keep that hostility alive.

Therefore I do not see, in attempting to bring about this peace through the means that I write of to you, greater difficulties than through those means of which you write; on the contrary, if there is an advantage, I see advantage in mine. On the other side, I do not see in your plan any

[3] Louis XII of France, who died in 1515.

safety, but in mine I do see some, of such a sort, though, as it is possible to get in these times.

He who wishes to see whether a peace is either durable or secure, must among other things find out who are discontented with it, and from their discontent what may emerge. So considering your peace, I see England, France, and the Emperor discontented, because not one of these has obtained his end. In mine, the discontented are England, the Swiss, and the Emperor, for the same reasons. The discontents of yours can easily cause the ruin of Italy and of Spain, because as soon as this peace is made, even though France has approved it and England has not rejected it, both of these two will again change their aim and their notion; and whereas France wished to go into Italy, and the other to master France, they will then turn to vengeance against Italy and against Spain. And reason requires that they make a second agreement between themselves, in which they will not have any difficulty in whatever they wish to do, when France is willing to reveal himself, because the Emperor with the aid of England and of France will leap the next day into Castile, will go into Italy when he wishes, will make France go there again, and so of a sudden these three together can upset and ruin everything. Neither the Spanish armies and the Swiss, nor the riches of the Pope are enough to hold this flood, because those three malcontents will have too much money and too many soldiers.

And it is reasonable that Spain should see these dangers, and that he should try in every way to escape them, because France in this peace has no cause for loving him, and much opportunity for damaging him; this opportunity France will be unlikely to give up in any way. Therefore if Spain has any eye at all for seeing things at a distance, he will not agree to it or carry it out, so that a peace will

be made which will stir up a war greater and more dangerous. But on making such a peace as I have written about,
in which the malcontents are England, the Emperor, and
the Swiss, these malcontents cannot, united or singly,
easily injure an alliance of the other three (the Pope,
France, Spain), because France, on this side and on the
other side of the mountains, will continue to be an ob-
stacle and, with the aid of the other two, will make such
opposition that the allies will be safe, and England and
the others will not undertake any enterprise, seeing its difficulty. And there will be nothing through which the allies
need to fear each other, since, as I have told you many
times, each of them will have carried out his intention,
and their enemies will be so powerful and dangerous as to
keep them chained together.

There is in your peace another very serious danger to
Italy, which is that every time there is a weak duke in
Milan, Lombardy will belong not to that duke but to
the Swiss. And though a thousand times those three (England, France, the Emperor) who are discontented at your
peace fail to stir, I believe the nearness of the Swiss is very
important and deserves to be more thoroughly considered
than it is. You say that the Swiss will not stir because
they have regard for France, because they will have the
rest of Italy against them, and because it will satisfy them
to give the country a raking[4] and go away. I cannot believe that you are right.

First, as I said above, France will desire to avenge
himself, and having received harm from all Italy, will delight in seeing her ruined. Therefore he will secretly give
the Swiss money, and feed this fire rather than otherwise.

As to union of the Italians, you make me laugh, first,
because there never will be union here to do anything
good. Even though the leaders should unite, they are not

<hr>

[4] Rapid plundering, as distinguished from serious occupation.

sufficient, because there are no armies here worth a farthing, except the Spanish, who, because they are few, are not enough. Second, because the tails are not united with the heads. The people of this generation will compete in submitting to the Swiss before they will move a step to use any opportunity that arises.

As to its being enough for the Swiss to give a raking and go away, I tell you not to rest on or encourage others to rest on such an opinion, and I beg you to consider how men's affairs develop, and how the powers of the world, and especially republics, have developed. You will see that at first it is enough for men to defend themselves and not to be mastered by others; from this they go on to injure others and to try to master others. For the Swiss it was at first enough to defend themselves from the dukes of Austria; this defense made them esteemed at home. Then it was enough to defend themselves from Duke Charles, which gave them a name away from home. Then it was enough for them to take stipends from others, in order to keep their young men ready for war, and to get honor. This has given them a still greater name, has made them bolder, because they have learned and observed more countries and more men, and also has put in their minds an ambitious spirit and a desire to try carrying on war for themselves. And Pellegrino Lorini said to me long ago that when they came with Beaumont to Pisa, they often talked among themselves about the efficiency of their military organization, and that it was like that of the Romans, and why could they not one day do as the Romans did? They were boasting that they had given France all the victories he had had up to that day, and that they did not know why one day they could not fight for themselves.

Now there has come this opportunity, and they have taken it, and they have entered Lombardy with the excuse of putting the present duke back there, but in fact they themselves are the duke. On the first opportunity they will become complete masters of Milan, destroying the ducal family and all the nobility of that state; on the second, they will overrun all Italy, producing the same effect. Therefore I conclude that it will not be enough for them to give a raking and go away; instead one needs to be exceedingly afraid of them.

I know that to this opinion of mine is opposed a natural defect of man: first, wishing to live from day to day; second, not believing that anything can happen that has not happened; last, always reckoning about a person in the same way. Therefore there will be no one who will advise us to consider getting the Swiss out of Lombardy in order to put the French back there, because they are not willing to run the present risks that must be run in attempting it, nor will they believe in future ills, nor will they dream of being able to trust France. My friend, this German river is so large that it has need of a great dyke to hold it. If France had never been in Italy, and you were not newly aware of the arrogance, satiety,[5] and extortion of the French, which are the things that upset this consideration for us, you would already have run to France to ask him to come into Lombardy, because the precautions against this flood need to be taken now, before the Swiss put down roots in this land, and commence to taste the sweetness of ruling. And if they settle themselves here, all Italy is ruined, because all the discontented will aid them, and make them a ladder for their own greatness and the ruin of others. And I fear them alone, and not them and the Emperor, as Casa has written to us, though it would be easy for them to unite, because, just as the Emperor has been pleased that they should overrun Lombardy and become lords of Milan, which would not

⁵ Probably a textual error.

seem reasonable in any way for the very reasons that you wrote to me, so, notwithstanding those, they might be content that he should make some progress in Italy.

Mr. Ambassador, I write more to satisfy you than because I know what I ought to say, and therefore I beg you that by your next letter you will advise me how this world stands, and what is being done, and what is hoped, and what is feared, if you wish that in these weighty matters I am to support my opinions. Otherwise you will get hold of an ass's will and testament, or some of those things, like Brancaccino. With my regards.

10 August 1513.

Niccolò Machiavelli, on his farm.

No. 133

25 August 1513, Florence
To Francesco Vettori

[Donato del Corno needs influence with the Medici]

Magnificent Ambassador:

Because I know how much you love our Donato del Corno,[1] and also he knows it, we have decided together with certainty to give you a bit of trouble, in order to see if by means of Signor Giuliano[2] we can satisfy him in this putting of his name in the bags that has to be done for the choice of officers.[3] You know with how much help Donato was assisted by the said Signor Giuliano in what he needed

[1] A Florentine of low rank but some wealth, often mentioned in the letters to Vettori.

[2] Giuliano de'Medici, Duke of Nemours, then residing in Florence.

[3] The bags contained the names of men considered eligible to hold office in Florence. When the offices were to be filled names were drawn out. The Medici government saw to it that only names acceptable to it were put in the bags.

to do in order to vote, which was in a certain way to the astonishment of everybody; which must result from the great love Giuliano has for him, or from great deserts. Now about these deserts I know something; and they are of such a sort that you or anybody might bring Donato's cause before His Lordship. And because we have done nothing, if there is no order that he be put in the bags and then recognized, it seems good to us now, since the couplers are engaged in putting names in the bags, to ask that Donato be put in. And therefore Donato writes the attached to His Lordship and reminds him simply of his idea, turning himself over to you for words; so that we beg you will be so good as to give His Lordship with your own hand the attached letter, and then to ask that he write instructing one or two couplers to put Donato in the bag among the first. I said two in order that there should be a clearer understanding of his will; but in whatever way he writes, the letter needs to indicate clearly that he wants it so, because you know the fussy people there are; and if it is not warm, we shall run into objections, and Donato will receive disgrace and harm. And because Donato trusts in M. Francesco Pepi, you might arrange that one of the two whom he writes should be Messer Francesco; and you might send the letter to Donato, so he can use it to his greatest advantage.

If I did not know how eager you are to help, and devoted to your friends, I would go to trouble in begging you, and so would Donato. May it be enough that he says he realizes that for the most part this benefit is from you. I am yours to command.

25 August 1513.

Your Niccolò Machiavelli, in Florence.

No. 134

26 August 1513, Florence
To Francesco Vettori

[See the head-note to Letter of 29 April 1513.]

[France, England, Spain, and above all the Swiss; Mercenary Soldiers]

Mr. Ambassador:

Your letter of the twentieth, now before me, bewildered me, because its arrangement, the multitude of its reasons, and all its other qualities so entangled me that in the beginning I was lost and confused; and if in the rereading I had not been a little reassured, I would have given you a bad card,[1] and would have answered you about other things. But as I get used to it, the same thing has happened to me as did to the fox when he saw the lion: the first time he was ready to die for fear; the second he stopped behind a bush to look at him; the third he spoke to him; and so having reassured myself by getting used to it, I shall answer you.

And as to the state of things in the world, I draw this conclusion about them: that we are ruled by princes of such a sort that they have, either by nature or by accident, these qualities: we have a Pope who is wise, and therefore serious and cautious; an Emperor unstable and fickle; a King of France inclined to anger and timid; a King of Spain stingy and avaricious; a King of England rich, fiery, eager for glory; the Swiss brutal, victorious, and arrogant; we

[1] Would not have replied.

in Italy poor, ambitious, cowardly; the rest of the kings I do not know about. Hence, considering these qualities in connection with what is going on at present, I believe the friar who said: "Peace, peace, and there will be no peace." [2] I admit to you that every peace is difficult, yours as well as mine. And if you hold that in mine there is more difficulty, I am satisfied; but I hope you will listen patiently, both where I imagine that you may be deceiving yourself, and where I feel sure that you are deceiving yourself.

Where I have doubts is, first, that you consider this King of France of little importance on too little evidence, and you make this King of England a great thing. To me it does not seem reasonable that France should not have more than ten thousand infantry, because from his own country, if he did not have Germans, he is able to get many, and if not as experienced as the Germans, they are as experienced as the English. What makes me believe it is that I see that this King of England with so much energy, with so large an army, with so much desire to tear him up by the roots, as the Sienese say, has not yet taken Therouanne, a fortified town like Empoli, at the first attack and in a time when his soldiers are acting with such great energy. This alone is enough for me not to have so much fear of England and not to put so low a value on France. And I judge that this caution by France is out of choice and not fear, because he hopes, England [3] not getting a foothold in that state and the winter coming on, that England will be forced either to return to his island or to remain precariously in France, since those places are swampy and without a single tree, so that the English must already have suffered much. And therefore I should suppose that it would not be very difficult for the Pope and Spain to influence England. Be-

---

[2] Savonarola.
[3] Here, as usually in Machiavelli, England, France, etc. mean the kings of those countries.

sides, that France has not decided to give up the Council makes me continue in the opinion given above, because if he were so much distressed, he would need everybody, and would wish to be on good terms with everybody.

As to the money that England has sent to the Swiss, I believe it, but I am astonished that he sent it by the Emperor's hands, because I should believe the Emperor would have wanted to spend it on his own soldiers, not on the Swiss. And I am not able to conclude that this Emperor is so thoughtless and the rest of Germany so careless as to allow the Swiss to rise to such influence. And when I see that it is so, I hesitate to judge anything, because this happens against every judgment a man can make. Not at all, too, do I know how it can be that the Swiss have held the Castle of Milan and have not wanted to, because to me it appears that, having it, their intention has been carried out; and that they ought to do this rather than go to take Burgundy for the Emperor.

Where I believe you deceive yourself entirely is in the affairs of the Swiss, about fearing them more or less. Because I judge that they are to be feared exceedingly; and Casa knows and many of my friends, with whom I am in the habit of talking about these things, know that I had a low opinion of the Venetians, even at their greatest strength, because I always thought it a much greater miracle that they gained that empire and held it than that they lost it. But their ruin was too honorable, because what was done by a king of France could have been done by a Duke Valentino or any general of reputation who had appeared in Italy and had commanded fifteen thousand persons. What moved me was their way of proceeding without generals and soldiers of their own.

Now those reasons that made me not fear them make me fear the Swiss. I do not know what Aristotle says about states made up of detached pieces, but I do consider what reasonably can be, what is, and what has been; and I remember reading that the Lucumnians held all Italy as far as the Alps, until they were driven from Lombardy by the Gauls. If the Aetolians and the Achaeans did not make progress, it resulted more from their times than from themselves, because they had always upon them a Macedonian king of the greatest power, who did not let them get out of their nest, and after him the Romans; so it was more the power of others than their own constitution that did not let them expand. Now, the Swiss do not wish to make subjects because they do not see in it their own advantage; they say so now, because they do not see it now; but, as I said to you about something else, things go along gradually, and often men are led by necessity to do what it was not their intention to do, and the habit of bodies of people is to go slowly. Considering where the matter stands, they already have in Italy as their tributaries a Duke of Milan and a Pope; this tribute they have put with their income, and they will not wish it to fail; and when the time comes that one of them does fail, they will consider it rebellion, and will be at once at their pikes, and winning the contest, they will consider making themselves safe, and to do this they will put some additional bridles on those they have conquered; and so little by little they will come to assert full authority.

Do not trust at all in those armies which you say will one day produce some fruit in Italy, because that is impossible. First, with respect to them, there would be many leaders and those disunited, and I cannot see that a leader can be found who will keep them united. Second, with respect to the Swiss. For you need to understand this: that the best armies are those of armed peoples; and they cannot be resisted except by armies similar to themselves. Remember some armies of renown: Romans, Lacedemonians, Athenians, Aetolians, Achaeans, swarms of Northerners. You see also that those who have done great things have armed their own people, as Ninus the Assyrians, Cyrus the Persians, Alexander the Macedonians. I find only Hannibal and Pyrrhus to represent those who with armies irregularly picked up have done big things. This came from the enormous ability of the leaders, and that was of such great influence that it gave their mixed armies the same spirit and discipline as are found in a ruler's own people.

And if you observe the defeats of France and his victories, you will see that he won as long as he fought against Italians and Spaniards, whose armies were like his own, but now that he has fought against armed peoples, such as the Swiss and the English, he has lost, and is in danger of losing more. And men of intelligence have always foreseen this calamity for France, inferring it from his not having his own infantry, and having disarmed his own people—which was contrary to every action and every precept of anyone who has been considered prudent and great. But this was not a defect of the early kings, but of King Louis, and from him on.

So do not, therefore, rely on Italian armies, if they are not either uniform like Swiss armies, or, being mixed, if they do not form one body like theirs.

And as to the divisions or disunions you mention, do not think they will produce an effect, so long as their laws are observed; and they are going to be observed for a while. Because in that land there cannot be or appear heads that have tails, and heads without tails are destroyed soon and produce slight effect. And those whom they have killed probably have been some who as magistrates or otherwise have wished in unusual ways to favor the French party, who have been found out and killed, and they are not more important in that state than a number here who are hanged as thieves.

I do not, indeed, believe they will produce an empire

like the Romans, but I do believe they can become masters of Italy, by reason of their nearness and our disorders and vile conditions. And because this frightens me, I wish to remedy it, and if France does not suffice, I see no other resource; and I am now ready to weep with you over our ruin and servitude, which, if it does not come today or tomorrow, will come in our time. And Italy will owe that to Pope Julius and to those who do not protect us, if protection can now be found.

Farewell. 26 August 1513, in Florence.

Niccolò Machiavelli.

No. 135

August 1513, Florence
To Francesco Vettori (a fragment)

[The character of Lorenzo de' Medici, Duke of Urbino[1]]

I do not wish to omit giving you notice of the Magnificent Lorenzo's way of proceeding, for he has demonstrated such quality up to now that he has filled with good hopes all this city, and it seems that everybody finds in him happy recollection of his grandfather; because His Magnificence is attentive to business, liberal and pleasant in audience, slow and weighty in his answers. The method of his conversing differs so much from that of the others that no pride is seen in it; yet he does not mix in such a way that through too great familiarity he gains a low reputation. With young men of his age, he has such a manner that he neither alienates them from himself nor does he give them

[1] Grandson of Lorenzo the Magnificent. At this time he was residing in Florence as a sort of prince. *The Prince* is dedicated to him.

confidence to indulge in any youthful insolence. He m
himself, in short, both loved and revered, rather i
feared, which as it is the more difficult to achieve, so it is
more praiseworthy in him.

The management of his house is so arranged that, though
we see there much splendor and liberality, nonetheless he
does not abandon the life of a citizen. Thus in all his move-
ments, outside and inside, nothing is seen that offends anybody or is to be censured; at which everybody appears to
be much pleased. And though I know that from many you
can learn this same thing, I have chosen to describe it, so
that from my account of it you can get that pleasure that
comes to all the rest of us, who continually experience it;
and you can when you have opportunity, give assurance of
it to his Holiness, our ruler.

No. 137

10 December, 1513, Florence
To Francesco Vettori, his benefactor.

[Niccolò's life on his farm; the composition of
The Prince; desire to serve the Medici]

Magnificent Ambassador:
"Never late were favors divine." [1] I say this because I
seemed to have lost—no, rather mislaid—your good will;
you had not written to me for a long time, and I was won-
dering what the reason could be. And of all those that came
into my mind I took little account, except of one only, when
I feared that you had stopped writing because somebody
had written to you that I was not a good guardian of your

[1] Petrarch, *Triumph of Eternity* 13.

letters, and I knew that, except Filippo and Pagolo,[2] nobody by my doing had seen them. I have found it again through your last letter of the twenty-third of the past month, from which I learn with pleasure how regularly and quietly you carry on this public office, and I encourage you to continue so, because he who gives up his own convenience for the convenience of others, only loses his own and from them gets no gratitude. And since Fortune wants to do everything, she wishes us to let her do it, to be quiet, and not to give her trouble, and to wait for a time when she will allow something to be done by men; and then will be the time for you to work harder, to stir things up more, and for me to leave my farm and say: "Here I am." I cannot however, wishing to return equal favors, tell you in this letter anything else than what my life is; and if you judge that you would like to swap with me, I shall be glad to.

I am living on my farm, and since I had my last bad luck, I have not spent twenty days, putting them all together, in Florence. I have until now been snaring thrushes with my own hands. I got up before day, prepared birdlime, went out with a bundle of cages on my back, so that I looked like Geta when he was returning from the harbor with Amphitryon's books.[3] I caught at least two thrushes and at most six. And so I did all September. Then this pastime, pitiful and strange as it is, gave out, to my displeasure. And of what sort my life is, I shall tell you.

I get up in the morning with the sun and go into a grove I am having cut down, where I remain two hours to look over the work of the past day and kill some time with the cutters, who have always some bad-luck story ready, about either themselves or their neighbors. And as to this grove I

---

[2] Filippo Casavecchia and Pagolo Vettori, brother of the recipient of the letter.

[3] A reference to a story founded on the *Amphitruo* of Plautus.

could tell you a thousand fine things that have happened to me, in dealing with Frosino da Panzano and others who wanted some of this firewood. And Frosino especially sent for a number of cords without saying a thing to me, and on payment he wanted to keep back from me ten lire, which he says he should have had from me four years ago, when he beat me at *cricca* at Antonio Guicciardini's. I raised the devil, and was going to prosecute as a thief the waggoner who came for the wood, but Giovanni Machiavelli came between us and got us to agree. Batista Guicciardini, Filippo Ginori, Tommaso del Bene and some other citizens, when that north wind was blowing, each ordered a cord from me. I made promises to all and sent one to Tommaso, which at Florence changed to half a cord, because it was piled up again by himself, his wife, his servant, his children, so that he looked like Gabburra when on Thursday with all his servants he cudgels an ox.[4] Hence, having seen for whom there was profit, I told the others I had no more wood, and all of them were angry about it, and especially Batista, who counts this along with his misfortunes at Prato.[5]

Leaving the grove, I go to a spring, and thence to my aviary. I have a book in my pocket, either Dante or Petrarch, or one of the lesser poets, such as Tibullus, Ovid, and the like. I read of their tender passions and their loves, remember mine, enjoy myself a while in that sort of dreaming. Then I move along the road to the inn; I speak with those who pass, ask news of their villages, learn various things, and note the various tastes and different fancies of men. In the course of these things comes the hour for din-

[4] Gabburra, apparently a butcher, is unknown.
[5] Batista Guicciardini was podestà of Prato when it was taken by the Spanish forces in 1512; as an immediate result the Medici were restored to Florence. It is remarkable that Machiavelli could jest about the fall of Prato and its attendant atrocities.

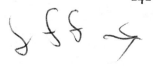

where with my family I eat such food as this poor
.. of mine and my tiny property allow. Having eaten, I
go back to the inn; there is the host, usually a butcher, a
miller, two furnace tenders. With these I sink into vulgarity
for the whole day, playing at *cricca* and at trich-trach, and
then these games bring on a thousand disputes and countless insults with offensive words, and usually we are fighting over a penny, and nevertheless we are heard shouting
as far as San Casciano. So, involved in these trifles, I keep
my brain from growing mouldy, and satisfy the malice of
this fate of mine, being glad to have her drive me along
this road, to see if she will be ashamed of it.

On the coming of evening, I return to my house and
enter my study; and at the door I take off the day's clothing,
covered with mud and dust, and put on garments regal and
courtly; and reclothed appropriately, I enter the ancient
courts of ancient men, where, received by them with
affection, I feed on that food which only is mine and which
I was born for, where I am not ashamed to speak with them
and to ask them the reason for their actions; and they in
their kindness answer me; and for four hours of time I do
not feel boredom, I forget every trouble, I do not dread
poverty, I am not frightened by death; entirely I give myself over to them.

And because Dante says it does not produce knowledge
when we hear but do not remember, I have noted everything in their conversation which has profited me,[6] and
have composed a little work *On Princedoms,* where I go as
deeply as I can into considerations on this subject, debating
what a princedom is, of what kinds they are, how they are
gained, how they are kept, why they are lost. And if ever
you can find any of my fantasies pleasing, this one should
not displease you; and by a prince, and especially by a

[6] This seems to be Machiavelli making notes on Livy's *History* for his
own *Discourses,* out of which rose *The Prince.*

new prince, it ought to be welcomed. Hence I am dedicating it to His Magnificence Giuliano.[7] Filippo Casavecchia has seen it; he can give you some account in part of the thing in itself and of the discussions I have had with him, though I am still enlarging and revising it.

You wish, Magnificent Ambassador, that I leave this life and come to enjoy yours with you. I shall do it in any case, but what tempts me now are certain affairs that within six weeks I shall finish. What makes me doubtful is that the Soderini we know so well are in the city, whom I should be obliged, on coming there, to visit and talk with. I should fear that on my return I could not hope to dismount at my house but should dismount at the prison, because though this government has mighty foundations and great security, yet it is new and therefore suspicious, and there is no lack of wiseacres who, to make a figure, like Pagolo Bertini, would place others at the dinner table and leave the reckoning to me.[8] I beg you to rid me of this fear, and then I shall come within the time mentioned to visit you in any case.

I have talked with Filippo about this little work of mine that I have spoken of, whether it is good to give it or not to give it; and if it is good to give it, whether it would be good to take it myself, or whether I should send it there. Not giving it would make me fear that at the least Giuliano will not read it and that this rascal Ardinghelli will get himself honor from this latest work of mine.[9] The giving of it is forced on me by the necessity that drives me, because I am using up my money, and I cannot remain as I am a long time without becoming despised through pov-

[7] Giuliano de'Medici, Duke of Nemours, son of Lorenzo the Magnificent. He resided in Florence after the restoration of the Medici in 1512, but in 1513 withdrew to Rome.

[8] Pagolo Bertini is unknown and the meaning of the sentence is uncertain.

[9] Piero Ardinghelli was secretary to Pope Leo X. Machiavelli seems to have feared that, if Giuliano had not read The Prince, Ardinghelli would steal ideas from it and offer them as his own.

erty.[10] In addition, there is my wish that our present Medici lords will make use of me, even if they begin by making me roll a stone; because then if I could not gain their favor, I should complain of myself; and through this thing, if it were read, they would see that for the fifteen years while I have been studying the art of the state, I have not slept or been playing; and well may anybody be glad to get the services of one who at the expense of others has become full of experience. And of my honesty there should be no doubt, because having always preserved my honesty, I shall hardly now learn to break it; and he who has been honest and good for forty-three years, as I have, cannot change his nature; and as a witness to my honesty and goodness I have my poverty.

I should like, then, to have you also write me what you think best on this matter, and I give you my regards. Be happy.

10 December 1513.

Niccolò Machiavelli, in Florence

No. 138

19 December 1513, Florence
To Francesco Vettori

[Donato del Corno's contribution to the Medici;
a Franciscan preacher]

Magnificent Ambassador:

I wrote eight or ten days ago, answering yours of the twenty-third of the past month, and told you, about my coming there, what kept me in doubt. I wait for your opinion and then I shall do what you advise.

The present letter I am writing to you in behalf of our

[10] A reminiscence of Juvenal 3.153 or Plautus, *Stichus* 1.3.20.

Donato del Corno.[1] You know how his affairs stand, and the letter that in the beginning he got from His Magnificence Giuliano to the Magnificent Lorenzo. Then there was the death of Messer Francesco Pepi, who had taken the affair on his shoulders, as a result of which Donato was almost deprived of hope. Yet, not to give up entirely, we went—Donato and I—to see Jacopo Gianfigliazzi, who promised us vigorously that he would leave nothing undone; and just two days ago, with the letter you wrote him, on this matter we spoke to him again, and he promised better than the first time, and concluded by saying that from now to the middle of January it could not be thought of, because he had to put the other names in the bags first. And on our asking if he advised getting further letters from Giuliano, he said such action could be only good, but that we should delay until the last in order to get the letter when the thing is to be done, because if he had it now, it would, when the time came, be old, and the business would have to be done over from the beginning. Yet we need to act so that at the right time we will have this letter; and if you had not got that of which you last wrote to Donato, you could let it go. If you had got it, we would need to consider at the time of action what ought to be done.

We think, relying on our first experience, that a letter, unless there is somebody here who will remember it, will be a dead favor. Hence we judge that you need to do something there, when you can, so that Ser Niccolò Michelozzi will receive this charge from Giuliano. Here he will remind Lorenzo of it, either through a letter that Giuliano will write him or through a letter that Piero Ardinghelli will write in Giuliano's name;[2] thus, whatever excuse Ser Nic-

[1] See Letter no. 133, above.
[2] As secretary to Pope Leo X, head of the Medici family, Ardinghelli could write in the name of Giuliano de'Medici, then probably in Rome, to Lorenzo de'Medici, duke of Urbino, in charge of the family interests in Florence.

colò may have, he will at the right time be made to remember the matter. And because we believe it will be easy for Piero Ardinghelli to attend to this thing, we suggest that you do some work on him, promising what you judge will be the best thing to offer him, and Donato will be generous about it. The way for this is open, because Piero knows that His Magnificence Giuliano has caused favors to be done to Maestro Manente and some others, whom Giuliano wished should be assisted, and so it is necessary that Donato get some favors. If Piero is willing, I believe we can get everything. So we think this medicine of Piero should be used, and that all the favors that are coming should come·from the eighth to the fifteenth of January, because Piero is at the business for the reasons given. And in order that you may know everything and see if Donato deserves to be put in the number of the loving servitors of the most illustrious Medici Family, you should know that about a day after they returned to Florence, Donato carried to His Magnificence Giuliano 500 ducats (it was lent to him freely and without its being asked for), for which he is still creditor.[3] This is not told you so that you will tell it to anybody, but so that, knowing it, you will undertake this affair with more spirit.

Donato and I are not trying hard to annoy you and re-annoy you in this matter, because, knowing how zealous a friend you are, we think by asking it to please you, and therefore he at the same time asks your aid and excuses himself to you, if it is at all necessary, and what we write we give as our opinion, but always we shall approve all the methods that you adopt as most prudent.

Those four verses that you write about Riccio in the beginning of the letter about Donato, we recited from memory to Giovanni Machiavelli; and in place of Machia-

[3] For Medici failure to repay this loan, see the letter of 17 Dec. 1517 (No. 166).

vello and Pera, we inserted Giovanni Machiavelli. As a result he has a head like a basket,[4] and says that he does not know where you have found anyone whom it would concern, and that he is going to write to you about it in any case, and for a while Filippo and I had a great deal of pleasure from it.

In this city of ours, which is a magnet for all the imposters in the world, there is a brother of Saint Francis who is half hermit, who, to get more belief for his preaching, claims to be a prophet, and yesterday morning in Santa Croce, where he preaches, he said many great and wonderful things: that before a long time passes, so that one who is ninety years old will be able to see it, there will be an unjust pope, set up against a just pope, and he will have his false prophets and will make cardinals, and will divide the church. Likewise, that the king of France is going to be utterly destroyed and one of the house of Rouen is to master Italy. Our city is to be given to fire and plunder, the churches will be abandoned and ruined, the priests dispersed, and three years we shall be without divine service. There will be pestilence and famine of the worst sort; in the city ten men will not be left, and on the farms two will not be left. There has been for eighteen years a devil in a human body and he has said mass. That some two million devils were unchained to be ministers of the things mentioned above, and that they entered into many bodies that died, and did not let those bodies decay, in order that false prophets and clergy might make the dead rise up, and be believed. These things frightened me yesterday to such an extent that I was going this morning to stay with *La Riccia*[5] and I did not go; but I do not at all know whether, if I had

---

[4] He is thoroughly confused.

[5] *La Riccia* (the rich woman) a Florentine harlot. *Il Riccio* (the rich man) is mentioned in the letter of 16 April 1513 (No. 122) as one of the servants of Donato del Corno. In a letter to Machiavelli, Vettori praises him as a faithful friend (9 Feb. 1513). The joke is not now clear.

had to stay with *il Riccio* I should have paid any attention to that Franciscan. The preaching I did not hear, because I am not given to such doings, but I have heard it reported in this way by all Florence.

I give you my regards and ask that you will greet Casa on my behalf, and tell him that if he does not follow other customs than he followed here, he will lose his credit with the fellows there as he has lost it here. Farewell.
19 December 1513.

Niccolò Machiavelli in Florence.

No. 140

5 January 1514, Florence
To Francesco Vettori . . . his most assiduous benefactor

[He who is held wise by day will never
be held crazy by night]

Magnificent Ambassador:

It is most certainly a great thing to consider how blind men are to the things in which they sin, and what sharp persecutors they are of the vices they do not have. I could bring up as examples things Greek, Latin, Hebrew, and Chaldean, and go off even to the land of the Sofi and Prester John, and bring them before you, if merely instances at home and recent were not enough. I believe Ser Sano[1] could have come into your house from one Jubilee to the next, and that never would Filippo have thought that he gave you any trouble. Instead he would have thought that you were glad to associate with him, and that it was

---

[1] According to Vettori's letters, some of his friends demurred at his association with this man.

just the habit suited to an ambassador, who, being obligated to countless serious doings, must necessarily have some recreations and pleasures; and this of Ser Sano would have appeared to him to fit exactly, and with everybody he would have praised your prudence and lauded you to the sky for such a choice. On the other side, I believe that if the whole brothel of Valenza had run through your house, Brancaccio never would have censured you for it; on the contrary he would have lauded you more for this than if he had heard you speaking before the Pope better than Demosthenes.

And if you had wished to see the proof of this reasoning, it would have been necessary for you, without either one's knowing of the admonitions of the other, that you should have given the appearance of believing them and wishing to carry out their advice. And if you had locked the door against the harlots and driven away Ser Sano, and drawn back to serious behavior and been immersed in thought, there would by no means have passed four days before Filippo would have said: "What has become of Ser Sano? What is the reason he doesn't come here any more? I believe him a respectable man; I don't know what those groups are chattering about, and I am sure he understands very well the habits of this court and is a useful thingamajig; you ought, ambassador, to send for him." About Brancaccio, I'm not saying whether he is grieved and astonished by the absence of the women, and if he wouldn't have said it to you, while he was keeping his arse turned to the fire, as Filippo would have done, he would have said it to you in your chamber when you were alone with him. And to explain this to you better, when you were in such a puritanical frame of mind, I, who associate with and pay attention to women, should have needed to come in there. As soon as I got a notion of the thing, I would have said: "Ambassador, you will get sick, and it does not seem to me that you have any recreation; here there are no boys; here there are no women; what sort of a bitchin' house is this?"

Magnificent Ambassador, there are none here except crazy men; and few there are who know this world, and who know that he who tries to act in the ways of others never does anything, because men never have the same opinions. These do not know that he who is thought wise by day will never be held crazy by night; and that he who is thought a man of substance, and effective, whatever he does to refresh his spirit and live happily will bring him honor and not blame; and instead of being called a bugger or a whoremaster, it will be said that he is tolerant, ready, and a good companion. They do not know also that he gives his own and does not take that of others, and that he acts like the must when it boils, which gives its flavor to dishes that smell of mould, and does not take mould from the dishes.

Therefore, Mr. Ambassador, do not be afraid of the mould of Ser Sano, nor of the rot of Mona Smeria, and follow your habits, and let Brancaccio talk; for he does not realize that he is one of those hedge birds that is the first to squawk and shriek, and then on the coming of the owl, is the first to be taken. And our Filippo is like a vulture, which when there is no carrion in the region, flies a hundred miles to find some; and when he has his crop full, he sits on a pine and laughs at the eagles, hawks, falcons, and the like, who since they eat delicate foods are for half the year almost dying of hunger. So, Magnificent Ambassador, let one squawk, and the other fill his crop, and you attend to your affairs in your own way.

In Florence, 5 January 1514.

Niccolò Machiavelli.

No. 142

4 February 1514, Florence
To Francesco Vettori . . . his benefactor.

[Amusement at Vettori's account of an evening in Rome]

Magnificent Ambassador:

I came back yesterday from my farm, and your Pagolo gave me your letter of the eighteenth of the past month, which answered one of mine of I don't know when, in which I took great pleasure, Fortune has been so loving to you that she arranged it so that Filippo and Brancaccio have with you become one soul in two bodies, or rather two souls in one body, in order not to make a mistake. And when I consider from the beginning to the end the story you have told of them and of yourself—which in truth, if I had not lost my trifles, I would have inserted among the recollections of modern things—it seems to me as worthy to be recited to a prince as anything I have heard this year.

It seems to me that I see Brancaccio curled up on a seat to sit low in order better to observe the face of Costanza, and with words and with signs, and with actions and with smiles, and movement of mouth and of eyes and of spitting, to be entirely poured out, entirely consumed, and completely hanging upon the words, upon the breath, upon the look, and upon the smell, and upon the sweet ways and womanly kindness of Costanza.

> I turned to the right hand, and saw Casa,[1]
> who with that boy was closer to the mark,
> a bit grave-looking, and with shaven head.

[1] Filippo Casavecchia.

I see him gesture, and now shift himself toward one side, now toward the other; I see him sometimes shake his head at the halting and modest answers of the boy; I see him, as he speaks with him, taking now the function of the father, now of the teacher, now of the lover; and that poor boy remaining doubtful of the end to which he wants to bring him; and now he fears for his honor, now trusts in the gravity of the man, now has respect for his elegant and mature bearing. I see you, Mr. Ambassador, at close quarters with that widow and her brother, and having an eye on that boy, the right however, and the other on that girl; and one ear for the words of the widow and the other to Casa and Brancaccio; I see you answering in general and to their last words, like Echo; and finally you cut off the talk and run to the fire with certain steps quick and long, with one bent finger on the small of your back. I see at your return Filippo, Brancaccio, the boy, the girl stand up; and you say: "Sit down, keep your seats, don't move, go on with what you were saying," and after many ceremonies, a little homely and slightly coarse, you get everybody seated and start some pleasant conversation. But above all I think I see Filippo when Piero del Bene came in; and if I knew how to paint, I would send him to you painted, because certain bold acts, forward acts, certain oblique glances, certain postures full of scorn cannot be described. I see you at table, I see the bread set out, the glasses, the table, and the trestles, and everybody showing, or rather dripping gladness, and at last all plunging into a flood of joy. I see in the end Jove chained in front of the chariot; I see you in love; and because when fire is applied to green wood it is more powerful, so the flame in you is greater because it has found more resistance. Here I should be permitted to exclaim with that man in Terence: "O heaven, O earth, O seas of Neptune!" I see you fighting within yourself, and since "Not easily go together or dwell in one place majesty

152

and love," [2] you would like to become a swan to lay an egg in her lap, now to become gold so that she might carry you off in her pocket, now one animal, now another, if only you are not separated from her.

And because you are terrified at my example, recalling what the arrows of love have done to me, I am forced to tell you how I have conducted myself with him. In short, I have let him go on and have followed him through valleys, groves, hills, and plains, and I have found that he has given me more pleasures than if I had treated him badly. Take off the pack-saddle then, pull out the bit, close your eyes, and say: "Go ahead, Love, guide me, lead me; if I come out well, may the praises be yours; if badly, may yours be the blame; I am your slave; you can gain nothing more by maltreating me, rather you will lose, maltreating your own property." And with such and like words, enough to bore through a wall, you can make him compassionate. So, my master, be happy; do not get frightened, show your face to Fortune, and continue to do those things that the revolutions of the heavens, the conditions of the times and of men bring before you, and do not doubt that you will break every snare and overcome every difficulty. And if you wish to make a serenade, I offer to come there with some fine invention to make her fall in love.

This is all that occurs to me in response to yours. About this place there is nothing to say, except prophecies and announcements of misfortunes, which God, if they speak falsely, I hope will cancel; if they speak the truth, I hope will turn to good.

When I am in Florence, I divide my time between the shop of Donato del Corno and la Riccia, and it seems to me I am boring both of them, for he calls me shop-nuisance, and she house-nuisance. Yet with both I conduct myself as a man of wisdom, and up to now I have profited so much

[2] Ovid, *Metamorphoses* 2.846.

153

from this reputation that Donato has let me get warm at his fire and the other lets me sometimes kiss her just in passing. I believe that this favor will last only a little while, because I have given both of them certain advice and they have never taken it, so that just today la Riccia said about me in a certain conversation that she was pretending to carry on with her servant: "These wise fellows, these wise fellows; I don't know where they live;[3] it seems to me that all of them take things by contraries."

Magnificent Ambassador, you see where the devil I am. Still I should like to keep these friends; but for myself I have no resource. If to you or to Filippo or to Brancaccio there occurs anything, I should be glad if you would write it to me. Farewell.

4 February 1514

Niccolò Machiavelli, in Florence.

No. 144

25 February 1514, Florence
To Francesco Vettori

[A Milesian tale of Florence]

Magnificent Ambassador:

I received a letter of yours week before last, and I have delayed until now in answering because I wished to learn better the truth of a story that I shall write below; then I shall answer parts of yours fittingly. An amusing thing has happened, or rather, to call it by its proper name, a ridiculous metamorphosis, and worthy to be set down in

---

[3] I don't understand how their minds work.

ancient writings. And because I do not wish anybody to complain of me, I shall relate it to you hidden under allegories.

Giuliano Brancaccio, for example, eager to go bird hunting, on one of the evenings of the past days, after the sounding of the Ave Maria in the evening, seeing the weather dark, the wind rising, and a little rain falling—each a sign for believing that all the birds would wait—returned to his house, pulled on his feet a pair of big shoes, strapped on a basket, took a fowling net, a little bell on his arm, and a good bird-swatter. He crossed the Bridge *alla Carraia,* and by way of the Canto de' Mozzi came to Santa Trinita, and having entered Borgo Santo Apostolo, went twisting around a bit in those alleys that surround it; and not finding birds that waited for him, turned toward your goldbeater, and near the Parte Guelfa crossed the Mercato and through the Calimala Francesca came under the Tetto de' Pisani, where looking carefully at all those hiding places, he found a little thrush, which with the bird-swatter and the light and the bell he stopped, and he cleverly brought it into the depth of the thicket near the cave where Panzano was living, and detaining his bird there, and having found its disposition generous, and many times having kissed it, he straightened two feathers of its tail, and at last, as many say, put it in the bird-basket hanging behind him.

But because the wind compels me to come out from under cover, and allegories are not enough, and this metaphor no longer serves me, Brancaccio wished to know who this was; and he answered, for example, that he was Michele, grandson of Consiglio Costi. Said at once Brancaccio: "Let it be a good omen; you are the son of a man of standing, and if you are wise, you have found your fortune. Understand that I am Filippo di Casavecchia, and I have a shop in such a place; and because I do not have money with me, either you come or you send tomorrow to the shop, and I'll pay you." When the morning came, Michele, who was rather bad than merely of little account, sent one Zanni to Filippo with a note asking him for what was due and reminding him of his promise. To that fellow Filippo showed an unpleasant air, saying: "Who is this, or what does he want? I have no connection with him; tell him to come to me." After that, Zanni having gone back to Michele and told him about it, the boy was not at all frightened, but boldly going to see Filippo, charged him with the favors he had received, and ended by saying that if Filippo did not hesitate to deceive him, he would not hesitate to speak ill of Filippo. Seeing that he was excited, Filippo took him into his shop and said to him: "Michele, you have been tricked; I am a man of good habits and do not indulge in such follies; so it is better to consider how you can find out about this trick, and that he who has had pleasure from you should pay you, than to take this road and without any benefit to yourself to speak ill of me. Therefore act in my way; go home, and tomorrow come to me and I'll tell you what I have decided on." The boy went off all confused; yet since he was to return, he remained patient. And when Filippo was alone, he was vexed by the strangeness of the thing, and without expedients, he fluctuated like the sea of Pisa when a hard south-west wind blows on it in the river mouth. Because he said: "If I keep still and satisfy Michele with a florin, I become his vineyard, make myself his debtor, confess the sin, and instead of innocent become guilty; if I deny it without finding out the truth of the thing, I have to stand in comparison with a boy; I have to justify myself to him; I have to justify myself to the others;[1] all the harm will be mine. If I try to find the truth, I must blame somebody for it; I might not hit it; I

---

[1] This seems the meaning, though the original says "to justify the others."

shall bring on hostility over it, and with it all I shall not be justified."

And being in this anxiety, as the least bad decision he took the last; and he was to such an extent favored by Fortune that the first aim he took was directed at the correct target; for he inferred that Brancaccio had done him that rascally deed, considering that he was one who did things under cover, and that at other times he had played him some tricks when he made a vow at the Servi. And he went thereupon to find Alberto Lotti, for example, and told him the affair, and gave him his opinion, and begged him to summon Michele, who was his relative, and see if he could find out anything. Alberto, as an active and perceptive man, judged that Filippo had a good eye, and having promised him his services freely, sent for Michele, and after sifting him a while came to this end: "Would you be sure, if you heard the man speak who said he was Filippo, that you could recognize him by his voice?" To which the boy having answered *Yes*, he took him to Santo Ilario, where he knew Brancaccio resorted, and coming up from behind, having seen Brancaccio, who was sitting in the middle of a big crowd telling stories, he managed that the boy got so close to him that he heard him speak; and on turning around and seeing him, Brancaccio, all confused, made off. So to everybody the affair seemed plain, in such a way that Filippo is now cleared and Brancaccio spoken ill of. And in Florence in this carnival nothing else is said than "Are you Brancaccio or are you Casa?" "And the story was well known under the whole heaven." [2] I believe you have had this account by other hands, but I wish to tell it more in detail, because so appears to me my obligation.

To your letter I have nothing to reply except that you should continue your love with loose reins, and the pleasure

[2] Ovid, *Art of Love* 2.561 (modified).

you take today, you will not have to take tomorrow; and
if the thing stands as you have written to me, I envy you
more than I do the King of England. I beg you to follow
your star, and not to let an iota go for the things of the
world, because I believe, have believed, and will believe
always that it is true, as Boccaccio said, that it is better to
act and repent than not to act and repent.
25 February 1514.

Niccolò Machiavelli, in Florence.

No. 145

16 April 1514, Florence
To Francesco Vettori.

[See the head-note to Letter of 29 April 1513.]

[Foreign powers in Italy; Swiss power;
Machiavelli's Finances]

Magnificent Ambassador, Francesco Vettori:
Will it be, then, after a thousand years, a reprehensible
thing to write something else than stories? I believe not.
And therefore I have decided, laying aside every irrational
hesitation, to beg you to straighten out for me a confusion I
have in my head.
I see the King of Spain, who, since he came into Italy,
has always been the first mover of all disturbances among
Christians, put in the middle, just now, of many difficulties.
It seems to me, first, that it does not advantage him that
Italy should continue with her present face, and that he
cannot bear that the Church and the Swiss shall have so
much power in her. He appears to have more fear about

the state of Naples now than when the French were there, because at that time the Pope was between Milan and Naples, for the Pope did not wish the French to get control of the Kingdom, in order not to be in the middle. But now between the Pope, the Swiss, and Spain there is no middle. It seems to me also that for things on the other side of the mountains to be in the midst of war does not advantage him, because not always can a war come out in a stalemate, as in the past year. And it would be necessary in the long run that the King of France should either win or lose; in neither of these lies the safety of Spain; so unless a third thing happens, so that the others are ruined, they all might turn to harming the cause of their trouble, because certainly Spain's tricks are known and they must have produced disgust and hatred in the minds of his friends and his enemies.

I conclude, then, that since things in their present state do not advantage him, it must be that he will try to change them. In attempting to change those of Italy with great safety, he must get the Swiss out of Milan, and not put France there. In this he has two difficulties: one that without France he cannot get the Swiss out; the other as to whom he can put there. Because, considering the first case, I do not believe that France ever will agree to come with all his forces into Lombardy except to be master. If there were agreements, either that he would come there, or would give Milan to the second son of King Philip, as his son-in-law, or to some other, I do not know how he would keep them, since his armies would be more powerful, if he were not always a ninny; and I do not see how Spain can trust in these promises. That the Swiss can be got out without France, I think everybody will say *No*, because, considering who they are, where they are, how many they are, and the purpose they have formed, anybody will judge that, without the French forces, they cannot be got out. As to the second difficulty, that of giving Milan to some one, to the Church I do not believe that he will give it, to the Venetians much less; for himself he cannot take her. He might give her, as I have said, to his grandson, as is more reasonable, yet there is no security for him there, because now that is the same thing as to give it to the Emperor; and when the Emperor saw himself ruler of Milan, he quickly would get the desire to be emperor of Italy, and would begin at Naples, where the Germans had a claim before the Spaniards.

So I see in Milan, when she is taken for the Archduke against the will of the Swiss, difficulties in holding her, especially without French weapons, because if the Swiss cannot resist the flood when it comes, they will let it pass, and when it is passed, they will come back there; because they know that if a duke does not keep always twenty thousand infantry and six thousand cavalry at least, he will never be safe from them; and to keep so many, Spain and the Emperor do not have resources. As a result the Swiss, notwithstanding the negotiations they learn are being held, which would result in giving that dukedom to the Archduke, stand firm against the French; and for these negotiations they show that they do not care, because they consider that others than the French cannot hold that dukedom against their will, and therefore they oppose the French, and the others they ridicule.

I should be glad, Mr. Ambassador, that you first would answer me, telling whether these presuppositions of mine seem to you true, and if they do, that you would solve them for me, and if you wish to understand my solution, I shall write to you at length very gladly.

The present officers of the *Monte*[1] are the Magnificent Lorenzo, Lorenzo Strozzi, Lorenzo Pitti, Ruberto de' Ricci, and Matteo Cini. They have not appointed officers for

[1] A body dealing with public finances.

sales; arrangement remains with them; and I have to come under their jurisdiction with nine florins of *decima,* and four and a half of *arbitrio,* so that in a year I run to forty florins and I have ninety as my income, or less. I worry along here as well as I can. If you think it wise to write a letter to any of these officials, and to assure them that my condition is impossible, I turn myself over to you. To the Magnificent there is no use in writing, because to that business he does not attend; it is enough to address one or two of the others.

16 April 1514.

Niccolò Machiavelli, in Florence.

No. 146

20 April 1514, Florence
To Giovanni Vernacci, in Pera.

[To a nephew in the cloth business in the Levant.]

[A marriage of convenience]

My dearest Giovanni:

I have your two letters of this last month, in which you instruct me to see to withdrawing that nun's money from the Monte, which task I shall perform, as soon as it is possible; because until after the octave of Easter, I cannot attend to it, because of its not being possible to see the ministry. I shall attend to it after that, and of the results I shall give you notice.

I shall find out from Lorenzo and others if I am able to turn any business to you, and if I can, shall let you know.

There is an artisan, a very rich man, who has one daughter a little lame, but otherwise beautiful, good, and worthy;

and in comparison with the other artisans he is of good
family, because he has the offices. I have thought that if he
would give you two thousand sealed florins ready money,
and promise to open for you a shop of the art of wool,
and make you active partner there, perhaps it would fit your
need, taking her as wife; because I believe he would ad-
vance to you 1500 florins, and that with those and with the
aid of your father-in-law, you would be able to get yourself
honor and profit. I have spoken of it in this way in general,
and have decided to write so you can consider it. Advise
me in your first letter, and if you like it, give me power
to act. Christ guard you.

In Florence, 20 April 1514.

Niccolò Machiavelli.

It would be possible to arrange to wait two or three years
before marrying her, if you wished to remain some time out
there.

No. 148

10 June 1514, Florence
To Francesco Vettori, in Rome.

[Machiavelli's finances; love]

Magnificent Ambassador:

I received your two letters when I was on my farm,
where I stay with my family, for Donato sent them to me
on behalf of Brancaccio. I made such reply as seemed suitable, both about my private affairs and about your love,
and other things. But coming two days ago to Florence, I
forgot them, so that since it seems to me a labor to rewrite
them, I shall send them to you at another time. And for

now I shall write to you this, in order that you may know that yours have arrived safely, and briefly I shall tell you that I have not gone to Rome, kept back by those causes that you now make clear to me, which I understood before for myself.

I shall remain, then, as I am, among my little affairs, without finding a man who remembers my service or who believes that I can be good for anything. But it is impossible that I can remain long in this way, because I am using up my money, and I see, if God does not show himself more favorable to me, that I shall be one day forced to leave home and hire out as a tutor or a secretary to a constable, since I can do nothing else, or fix myself in some desert land to teach reading to boys, and leave my family here, which could reckon that I am dead, and would get on much better without me, because I am an expense to them, being used to spending, and unable to get on without spending. I do not write this because I want you to undertake for me something troublesome or annoying, but merely to express myself and in order not to write more of this matter, which is as hateful as it can be.

About your love, I remind you that the only ones who are tortured by love are those who, when he flies into their bosoms, try to clip his wings or bind him. To such, because he is a boy and unsettled, he digs out their eyes, their liver, and their heart. But those who, when he comes, are pleased and caress him, and when he goes away let him go, and when he comes back, receive him gladly, he always honors and holds dear, and under his command they triumph. Therefore, my friend, do not try to regulate one who flies, or to clip one who returns a thousand feathers for one; and you will be happy.
10 June 1514.

Niccolò Machiavelli.

No. 150

3 August 1514, Florence
To Francesco Vettori

[Niccolò's new love, probably fictitious]

You, my friend, have with many accounts of your love at Rome kept me all rejoicing, and you have removed from my mind countless worries, through my reading and thinking of your pleasures and your angers, because one is not good without the other. And truly Fortune has brought me to a place where I can render you just recompense for it, because being at my farm I have encountered a creature so gracious, so delicate, so noble, both by nature and environment, that I cannot praise her so much or love her so much that she would not deserve more. I ought to tell you, as you did me, the beginning of this love, with what nets he took me, where he spread them, of what sort they were; and you would see that they were nets of gold, spread among flowers, woven by Venus, so pleasant and easy that though a villainous heart might have broken them, nonetheless I did not wish to, and for a bit I enjoyed myself in them, until the tender threads became hard and secured with knots beyond untying.

And you should not believe that Love, in order to take me, has used ordinary methods, because knowing that they would not have been enough for him, he used extraordinary ones, of which I knew nothing, and from which I could not protect myself. May it be enough for you that, already near fifty years, neither do these suns harm me, nor do rough roads tire me, nor the dark hours of the night frighten me.

Everything to me seems level, and to all her desires, even though unlike mine and opposed to what mine ought to be, I adapt myself. And though I seem to have entered into great labor, nevertheless I feel in it such sweetness, both through what that face so wonderful and soft brings me, and also through having laid aside the memory of all my troubles, that for anything in the world, being able to free myself, I would not wish it. I have abandoned, then, the thoughts of affairs that are great and serious; I do not any more take delight in reading ancient things or in discussing modern ones; they all are turned into soft conversations, for which I thank Venus and all Cyprus.[1] So if it occurs to you to write anything about the lady, write it, and of the other things talk with those who estimate them higher and understand them better, because I never have found in them anything but harm, and in these of love always good and pleasure. Farewell.

From Florence, 3 August 1514.

Your Niccolò Machiavelli.

No. 152

4 December 1514, Sant'Andrea in Percussina
To Francesco Vettori.

[The marriage troubles of a friend's sister]

Magnificent Ambassador:

The presenter of these words will be Nicholas Tafanus, my friend. The cause of his journey is his sister, whom some time ago he gave over in matrimony to a certain Giovanni; he was held by the bond of a ring; and yet rejecting all

---

[1] The island of Cyprus was the realm of Venus.

oaths, and despising the laws of marriage, he went to Rome, where for a long time he has lived and still lives, paying no attention to his marriage and his wife. Therefore this my friend wishes one of these two things: either that Giovanni should join his wife here or, returning the portion of dower he received, should legally repudiate her, for he judges all such things can easily be done there where the Vicar of Christ lives. In this matter, therefore, we ask your aid and ask that you will approach that disloyal husband, and with such authority as you can, force him to satisfy the two Niccolòs who so heartily ask it. I am moved both by justice, which strengthens our case, and by the eagerness of the man himself and of his whole family, than which nothing in this rural region is pleasanter to me.

But enough on Tafanus. As to what pertains to me, if you wish to know what I am doing, you can learn from this same Tafanus the whole course of my life, and will realize how sordid and inglorious it is—not without anger, if as in the past you love me. For this I suffer and lament the more when I see that amid so many and so great instances of prosperity for the Magnificent Family and for the city, to me alone Troy remains.[1]

From Percussina, 4 December 1514.

Niccolò Machiavelli.

No. 154

20 December 1514 (Letter No. 1), Florence
To Francesco Vettori.

[See head-note to Letter of 29 April 1513.]

[1] Ovid, *Metamorphoses* 13.507. Machiavelli expected his friend to cap the quotation, which continues: My woe still runs its course.

[The wisest policy for the Pope is a French alliance;
the Swiss as rulers of Italy; neutrality]

You ask me what decision His Holiness Our Lord should
make in order to keep the Church in the position of influence where he found her, since France with the assistance of England and the Venetians wishes by all means
to recover the state of Milan, and on the other side the
Swiss, Spain, and the Emperor unite to defend it. This
is really the most important of your questions, because
all the others depend on it, and they must be explained if
this one is to be explained properly. I do not believe that
for twenty years there has been a more serious question
than this, nor do I know a thing among those past so
difficult to understand, so uncertain to judge, and so dangerous to decide and carry out; yet, being forced by you,
I will enter into this matter, discussing it honestly at
least, if not adequately.

When a prince wishes to know what is going to be the
fortune of two who fight each other, he must first measure
the forces and the vigor of both. The forces, in this matter
of France and of England, are those preparations that
those kings are said to have made for this conquest, namely,
to attack the Swiss in Burgundy with twenty thousand
men, to attack Milan with a greater number, and with a
much greater number to attack Navarre, in order to cause
rebellion and change in the states of Spain; to put a great
fleet on the sea and attack Genoa or the Kingdom, or
wherever it may be to their advantage. These preparations
which I mention are possible for these two kings and, if
they intend to win, necessary; and therefore I suppose
them true. And though it is in your last question, and it is
possible to think that England will detach himself from
France, being displeased by his greatness in Italy, I

prefer to debate this matter now, because if England detaches himself from him, every question will be answered.

I believe that the reason why England sticks with France is to avenge himself on Spain for the injuries done to him in the French war; which anger is reasonable, and I do not see anything that so quickly could cancel this and destroy the love of the marriage contracted between those two kings; and I am not moved by the ancient hostility between the English and the French, which moves many, because the people wish what the kings do, and not the kings what the people do. As to his being caused annoyance by the power of France in Italy, evidently this must be the result either of envy or of fear. Envy could appear if England too did not have a place where he could get honor, and would have to remain idle, but when he can make himself famous in Spain, the cause of the envy ceases. As to fear, you must understand that many times a ruler gains territory but not forces, and if you consider well, you will see that for the King of France the gaining of cities in Italy is, with respect to England, a gaining of territory and not forces; because with as large an army he could attack that island without the states of Italy as with them; and as to diversions because France has Milan, England no longer needs to fear France, who has a disloyal state, and there is nothing to prevent England from moving the Swiss against him by paying them, for they, being injured by France, would be truly his enemies, and not as the other time. And because it also could happen, while France was gaining Milan, that England would upset the state of Castile, England with that conquest might harm France more than France could harm him with the conquest of Milan, for the reasons given. Therefore I do not see why England in this first rush of the war should need to detach himself from France, and therefore I affirm these unions and preparations of forces mentioned above to be necessary and possible.

We have remaining the Venetians, who are of the same importance to the forces of these two kings as are the forces of Milan to that other side; I judge them few and weak, and to be held back by half of the soldiers who are in Lombardy. Considering now the defenders of Milan, I see the Swiss in condition to put two armies together that can fight with any French that may come into Burgundy, and with those who come against Italy, because if in this case all the Swiss unite, and with the cantons are joined the Grisons and the Vaudois, they can bring together more than twenty thousand men to an army.

As to the Emperor, because I do not know what he will do at any time, I do not care to discuss what he can do now. But uniting Spain, the Emperor, Milan, and Genoa, I do not believe they can raise more than fifteen thousand men fit for war, Spain not being able to furnish new forces, because of expecting war at home.

As to the sea, if they do not lack money, I believe that between the Genoese and Spain they can form a fleet that to some extent can delay that of their opponents. I believe, then, that these are the forces of the two.

Trying at present to see to which side victory may incline, I say that the two kings, being moneyed, can for a long time keep their armies together; the others, being poor, cannot. Hence, considering the armies, the condition, and the money of the two, I believe it can be said that if they come quickly to a battle, the victory will be on the side of Italy; if the war drags on, that it will go to the other side. It is said, and seems reasonable, that the Swiss, knowing this difficulty, and in order to come to battle quickly, intend to meet the French armies on the mountains of Savoy, in order that the latter, if they try to cross, will be forced to fight or, if they do not fight, to turn back, because of the narrowness of the position and the lack of supplies. Whether in this they are likely to succeed, would have to be judged by someone experienced in the region and in war.[1] Nevertheless, I shall say this: that never in ancient history have I found that anyone has succeeded in holding the passes; but I have surely seen many who have left the passes and waited for the enemy in open places, judging that they could better defend themselves, and with less disorder tempt the fortune of war—all their fortune and not all their forces.[2] And though I might give some reasons showing why this is, I prefer to omit them, since this subject does not demand their discussion.

Considering everything, then, I see on this side the single hope of coming to a battle quickly, which also might be lost. On the side of France, I see him likely to win the battle, and, by dragging out the war, unable to lose it; and I see on this side, among others, in the management of the war two obvious perils: one that the French with their fleet, either by force or by treaty, will come into the territory of Genoa or into Tuscany, where they will no sooner land than all the province of Lombardy will be theirs; and many others, some of them timid and some discontented, will run to join them, in such a way that the French, finding that they are received, can dally with and wear out the Swiss at their pleasure. The other danger is that those cantons that are on the borders of Burgundy, on whom will fall the weight of the war made in those regions, if they see it last too long, will force

[1] In 1515 the usual passes were guarded against the French. They suddenly crossed by an unusual one that was left unguarded, to the consternation of their adversaries. In this instance Machiavelli was a prophet.

[2] So the detached words as they stand in all texts must be rendered. At least it is plain that Machiavelli is referring to his belief that a ruler should not risk all his fortune when using only part of his forces. See *Discourses* 1.23.

the others to make peace with France. I am led to fear this by the example of Charles duke of Burgundy who, by making war and raiding on that side, to such an extent tired them out that they sent him a blank sheet of paper, and he would have ruined them entirely if he had not been suddenly forced into battle. And whereas some hope or fear that the Swiss through their disloyalty will turn and make agreements with England and France, and give the others up as booty, I do not fear it, because they are fighting now for their own ambition; and if there is not one of the aforesaid necessities that compels them, I believe that in the war they will be loyal.

If then His Holiness the Pope is forced to make a decision, and should choose the party on this side, I see the victory doubtful for the reasons given above; both because his joining them does not make them altogether certain, and because if it does take away convenience and influence from the French, it does not give the others forces enough to enable them to hold the French. Indeed, since the King has a great fleet on the sea and the Venetians also can arm some ships, it will be so difficult for the Pope to guard his shores above and below[3] that his soldiers and yours here will scarcely be enough. It can happen, it is true, that His Holiness will escape a present danger, if they wish to make themeselves sure of him, and will find also a present profit, since at present he can honor his friends.

If His Holiness takes the side of France, provided he does it so cautiously that he can without danger wait for France, I judge victory sure, because, by means of the fleet, he can put in Tuscany a great army along with his own. Thus he would at once cause a great uproar in Lombardy by acting with the Venetian soldiers there. The Swiss and the Spaniards could not resist two different

[3] The Adriatic and the Mediterranean.

armies from different sides and defend themselves from the rebellion of the people, which would be instantaneous. Altogether I do not see that it would be possible to deprive the King of victory.

You wish, besides, to learn which would be less burdensome to the Pope: alliance with the French or with the Swiss, if either one could win with his alliance. I answer that I believe the Swiss as victors and their associates and allies, if they conquer, would at present observe an agreement with the Pope, and would give him his states. But on the other hand he would have to bear the arrogance of the victor; and because I should not recognize as victors any but the Swiss, he would have to bear their injuries, which would be of two sorts: first, they would deprive him of money; second, of friends. Because the money that the Swiss say they do not want now, when they are carrying on the war, you may believe they will be sure to want when it is finished, and they will begin with some tax, which will be heavy, and in order to appear honest, and for fear of irritating them in the first heat of their victory, it will not be denied to them. I believe, rather I am certain, that the Duke of Ferrara, the Lucchese, and the like, will run to make themselves their dependents. When the Swiss have taken one of them, it will be all over with Italy's liberty, because every day with a thousand excuses they will tax and plunder, and they will change governments, and what they judge they cannot do now, they will put off until there comes a time to do it. Nor should anybody assure himself that they do not think of this, because they must think of it, and if they do not think of it, they will be made to think of it by the course of events; for the truth is that one conquest, one victory, causes thirst for another.

No one should be astonished that they have not taken Milan openly, and have not gone farther than they have, because the method of their procedure, as at home it is unlike others, so it is unlike away from home, and has its parallel in all the ancient histories; because if up to now they have made for themselves associates, in the future they will make for themselves dependents and tributaries, not troubling to command them or to manage them in details, but it is enough only that they hold by them in wars and that they pay them the annual tribute; these things the Swiss will keep up with the reputation of their armies at home and by punishing those who deviate from them. In this way, and quickly, if they keep up this war, they will give laws to you, to the Pope, and to all other Italian princes, and when you see that they assume a protectorate, "you may know that the summer is at hand." [4] And if you say: "For that there will be a cure, because we shall unite against them," I say that this will be a second error and a second deception, because the union of many leaders against one is difficult to bring about, and once made, is difficult to maintain.

I give you as an example France, against whom everybody had entered into an alliance; but suddenly Spain made a truce, the Venetians became his friends, and the Swiss attacked him feebly; the Emperor was not seen again, and finally England joined with him. Because if that man against whom an alliance is made is of so much vigor that he does not at once go up in smoke, as the Venetians did, he always finds his advantage in many opinions,[5] as France has done, and as we see the Venetians would have done if they could have kept up that war for two months. But their weakness could not await the disunion of the allies, something that would not happen to the Swiss, who always would find, either with France, or with the

<hr>

[4] Matthew 24.32.
[5] The conflicting opinions of allies each of whom is seeking his own advantage.

Emperor, or with Spain, or with the potentates of Italy, a way either to keep them all from uniting, or if they did unite, to disunite them. I know that at this opinion many will poke fun, and I fear it so much and so much believe it that, if the Swiss succeed in checking this flood, and we both live seven years, I expect to remind you of it.

Since you wish to know what the Pope has to fear from the Swiss if they win when he is their ally, I say that he must fear some immediate taxes and, in a short time, servitude for himself and for all Italy without hope of redemption, since they have a republic, armed beyond comparison with any prince or potentate. But if he were the ally of France, and should win, I believe France would still keep his agreement, if the conditions were suitable and if too much eagerness had not made the Pope ask too much and the King yield too much. I believe he would not lay tribute on the Church but on you,[6] and that he would have consideration for her on account of his alliance with England, and on account of the Swiss, who would not all be dead, and on account of Spain, who, even though driven out of Naples, would be of some importance as long as he lived. Therefore it seems reasonable that France for his part would wish the Church influential and friendly, and also wish the Venetians so. Altogether, in any outcome of these victories, I see that the Church must be in some one's power; therefore I judge it better to be in the power of those who will be most reasonable and whom she knows from other times, and not in the power of those whose wants she does not know, since she does not know them well.

If the side to which His Holiness Our Lord adheres should lose, I fear his being brought into every extreme necessity of flight and of exile and of everything that a pope can fear. Therefore when a prince is forced to take

[6] The Florentines.

one of two courses, he ought, among other things, to consider where the bad fortune of either of these can bring him, and always ought, other things being equal, to take that course which in its end, if it is bad, will be least bitter. Without doubt loss would be less bitter with France as an ally than with the others as allies; because if His Holiness has France as ally, and loses, he has left the country of France, which is able to uphold a Pontiff's honor; he remains with a fortune that through the power of that kingdom can rise up in many ways; he remains in his own house, and where many popes have had their seat.[7] If he is with those others and loses, he will need to go either into Switzerland to die of hunger, or into Germany to be laughed at, or into Spain to be swindled, so that the evil brought on by the bad fortune of one is not to be compared with that from the other.

As to remaining neutral, I do not believe that it was ever of profit to anybody, when he is in these conditions, namely, when he is less powerful than any of those who are fighting, and when his states are scattered among the states of those who are fighting. And you must realize, first, that there is nothing more necessary to a prince than to govern himself in such a way in dealing with his subjects and with his allies and neighbors, that he does not become either hated or despised; and if indeed he must neglect one of these two, he should not pay attention to hatred but should look out for contempt. Pope Julius did not trouble about being hated, if only he was feared and respected; and by means of that fear he turned the world upside down and brought the Church where she is. And I say that he who remains neutral is sure to be hated by him who loses and despised by him who wins; and as one who is thought of no account and considered a useless ally and an undreaded enemy, he needs to fear that every

[7] At Avignon.

sort of injury will be done him, and every sort of destruction will be planned for him. And the victor will never lack justification, because the neutral prince, with his states mixed among those at war, is forced to receive into his gates now this one, now that, to receive them into his house, to aid them with shelter, with food; and always everyone will imagine he is being deceived, and there will happen countless things that will cause countless complaints. And even though in the carrying on of the war nothing comes up—which is impossible—it will come up after the victory, because the lesser powers, and those who fear you, run quickly to the shelter of the victor, and give him opportunity to hurt you; and to him who says: "It is true that one thing can be taken away from us and another thing left to us," I answer that it is better to lose everything nobly than a part shamefully, and a part cannot be lost without the whole's tottering. He who considers therefore all the states of His Holiness our Lord, and where they are, and of what sort are the lesser powers included in them, and who they are who are fighting, will judge His Holiness to be one of those who in no way can continue such neutrality, and that he would be forced, making such a choice, to be hostile to him who wins and to him who loses, and that everybody would wish to harm him, one for vengeance and another for profit.

You also ask me if, when the Pope allies himself with the Swiss, the Emperor, and Spain, it would advantage Spain and the Emperor to deceive him and join France. I believe that a treaty between Spain and France is impossible and that it cannot be made without England's consent, and that England cannot consent except to attack France; for that reason France could not think of it, because the English king, being young and eager for war, has nowhere to go with his armies except into France or into Spain, and as peace with France would bring war upon Spain, so peace with Spain would bring war upon France. Therefore the King of France, in order not to lose England, in order not to bring upon himself that war, and having a thousand reasons for hating Spain, is not going to give ear to peace; for if France wished or was able to make it, it would have been done—so many plans for the damage of others that king could have brought forward. So that as far as Spain is concerned, I believe that the Pope would have reason to fear everything; but so far as France is concerned, he would be safe. And as to the Emperor, since he is shifting and unstable, every change is to be feared whether it would advantage him or would not advantage him, since in these variations he has always lived and been nourished. If the Venetians should join this party here, it would be of great moment, not so much because of the addition of their forces as through this group's remaining more simply an enemy of France, and if the Pope also joined it, there would be for the French, both in coming and in establishing themselves in Italy, countless difficulties. But I do not believe the Venetians will adopt this plan, because I believe they have had better terms from France than they have had from these others, and having followed a French Fortune when she was almost dead, it does not seem reasonable that they will abandon her now that she is about to rise up again, and I fear that they are offering empty words, as they usually do, for their own advantage.

I conclude, then, to come to the end of this discourse, that since there are more indications of victory on the French side than on that of the others, and since the Pope by joining can give the victory to France with certainty, and not to these others, and France is less to be feared and more bearable as friend and conqueror than these others, and loss is less hard with France as ally than with these others, and since he cannot securely remain neutral, that

His Holiness our Lord ought either to join France, or to join the others if the Venetians also join them, and not otherwise.

20 December 1514.

No. 155

20 December 1514 (No. 2), Florence
To Francesco Vettori, in Rome

[See head-note to Letter of 29 April 1513.]

[More on neutrality]

Magnificent Ambassador:

Since you have inspired my strong desire, if I weary you with writing, say: "Let the injury be my own, since I wrote to him." I fear you will think that in my reply to your questions I passed too hastily over that part on neutrality; and also that where I had to debate what he would have to fear from the conqueror if that party which he joined should lose, because in both it seems there are many things to consider. So I have made a stab at writing to you again. And as to neutrality, a choice that many seem to approve, it cannot please me, because I do not recall, either in those things I have seen or in those I have read, that it has ever been good, rather that it has always been very injurious, because it is certain to lose; and though you understand the reasons better than I do, yet I am going to recall them to you.

You know that the chief duty of every prince is to keep himself from being hated and despised, to avoid in his conduct contempt and hatred; whenever he does that well, everything must go well. And this matter he must practice as much with his allies as with his subjects; and whenever a prince does not avoid at least contempt, he is done for.

To me it seems that to remain neutral between two who are fighting is nothing else than to seek to be hated and despised, because always there will be one of them to whom it will appear that, by reason of benefits received from him or through long-standing alliance with him, you are obligated to follow his fortune, and when you do not join him, he at once hates you. That other despises you, because he finds you timid and irresolute, and quickly you get to be known as a useless friend and a harmless enemy, so that whoever conquers harms you without hesitating. And Titus Livius in a few words (as from the mouth of Titus Flaminius) gives this opinion, when he said to the Achaians, who were exhorted by Antiochus to remain neutral: "Nothing is farther from your interests; without favor, without dignity, you will be the booty of the winner."

It is also inevitable that in the conduct of the war between these two, countless reasons for hate against you will appear; because most of the time the third is put in such a place that he can in many ways hinder or help one or the other. And always in a short time, beginning with the day when the war is started, you are brought to such a pass that the declaration you have not been willing to make openly and with credit, you are obliged to make secretly and without thanks; and if you do not do it, some still believe that you *have* done it. And when Fortune is so generous in favor of the neutral that in the conduct of the war there rises no just cause for hatred on the part of either belligerent, it must appear when the war is ended, because all those who have been injured by him who has been third,[1] and all those afraid of him, running to the shelter of the victor, give him cause for hatred and discord with you.

And if somebody answers that the Pope, through the reverence felt for his person and through the authority of the Church, is in another situation, and will always have a

[1] The neutral.

refuge in which to save himself, I answer that such a reply deserves some consideration, and that there it is possible to build on some foundation. Nevertheless it is not to be relied on; on the contrary I believe that, if he is to be well advised, it is not to be thought of, so that such a thought will not cause him to make a bad choice. Because all the things that have been can, I believe, be again; and I know that pontiffs have fled, gone into exile, been pursued, suffered to the utmost, like temporal rulers, and this in times when the Church in spiritual matters was more revered than she is today.

If His Holiness our Lord will consider where his states are situated, who they are who are fighting together, who they are who can take refuge with the winner, I believe then His Holiness will not at all rest neutral, and that he will think that it advantages him more to join, no matter what, so that, as to neutrality, to explain it at greater length than the other time, I have nothing more to say to you. And as to what he would have to fear from him who would win the victory and conquer that party which he had joined, I shall say nothing further about it, because I have said it all above.

I believe you may infer from the letter I wrote you that I would depend on France; anybody who read it would fear that affection had influenced me to some extent. That would displease me, because I try always to keep my judgment firm, especially in these matters, and try to let it be uncorrupted by a vain contest, as do many others; and because, if I have depended somewhat on France (I think I have not been deceived), I wish again to run over what moved me, which will form a sort of epilogue to what I have written.

When two potentates fight together, in order to judge who is likely to win, it is necessary, besides measuring the forces of the two, to see in how many ways the victory can come to one and in how many to the other. I see nothing for the party on this side to do except come to battle quickly; but for the French party there are all the other methods, as I wrote at length. This is the first reason that makes me believe more in France than in the others. Besides, if I have to declare myself ally to one of the two, and I see that by joining one I give him the victory with certainty, and by joining the other I give it to him doubtfully, I believe that it will always be right to take the certain, laying aside every obligation, every interest, every fear, and every other thing that may displease me. And I believe that if the Pope joins the French, there will be no dispute on this; but if he joins those others there will be plenty of dispute, for those reasons that just now I wrote to you. Besides this, all wise men, when it is possible for them not to gamble all their property, are glad of the chance, and considering the worst that can come of it, they think where in the evil before them the smallest evil appears. And because the things of Fortune are all doubtful, they pursue willingly that Fortune who, doing the worst she can, will bring about the least unpleasant result.

His Holiness our Lord has two dwellings, one in Italy, the other in France. If he joins France, he risks one of them, if the others, he risks both. If he is an enemy to France and France wins, he is obliged to follow the Fortune of these others, and to go into Switzerland to die of hunger, or into Germany to live in despair, or into Spain to be swindled and turned into profit. If he joins France and loses, France remains to him, he lives in his dwelling, and with a kingdom at his service that is a papacy, and with a prince who, either through treaty or through war, may in a thousand ways rise up again. Farewell. And a thousand times I greet you.

20 December 1514.

Niccolò Machiavelli, in Florence.

20 December 1514 (No. 3), Florence
To Francesco Vettori

[Donato's affairs, and Niccolò's own]

Magnificent Ambassador:

When I had written the attached, I received yours of the fifteenth, which I will answer only in the part pertaining to Donato, to whom I read the section; and at once he was so blown up with hope that his shirt doesn't touch his enterprise.[1] Because he has decided that in order to obtain this favor he will not be stingy in anything, he had the letter to Beni rewritten, through which, inside of six months, there will be paid to you when you wish a hundred ducats. And he has said to me that, besides these, when you need others, you should not spare anything or have regard to anything. The letters will be included in this; you will make use of them when convenient[2] and as is usual for such letters. About being sparing with them or not, Donato did not wish me to write anything, yet as from myself I bring it to you, especially since the act of a friend does not need more in any way; if there is nothing more to be written in this affair, I suppose it can neither hinder nor help. Yet Donato does not wish that this be thought of, or that anything be regarded, if only once he can get out of the plebeian class.

I thank you again for all the work and all the thoughts you have had for love of me. I do not promise you any

---

[1] Apparently bowdlerized by an editor.
[2] Some texts leave a blank at this point.

recompense for it, because I do not believe I can ever do good either to myself or to others. And if Fortune had wished that the Medici, either in affairs in Florence or abroad, or in their private business or in that of the public, had once employed me, I should be satisfied. Nevertheless, I do not yet really doubt myself. When this happens and I do not know how to sustain myself, you may grieve for me; but that which has to be, let it be. And I realize every day that what you say Pontanus writes is true; "and when Fortune decides to please us, she puts before us either present utility or present fear, or both together;" which two things I believe are the greatest enemies of that opinion I have defended in my letters.[3] Farewell.
20 December 1514.

Niccolò Machiavelli.

No. 159

31 January 1515, Florence
To Francesco Vettori, in Rome

[Grave men at leisure; the new prince]

The boyish archer had already many times attempted to wound my breast with his arrows, for in hatred and in the injury of others he takes pleasure.

And though they were, those arrows, so sharp and biting that adamant would not have warded them off, nonetheless they struck so strong an object that I little regard all their power.

He then, possessed with anger and fury, in order to show his lofty power, changed quiver, changed bow, and arrow; and he shot one with such great force that I still feel the

---

[3] They are opposed to the courage and prudence that can resist and even overcome Fortune.

pain of its wound, and I confess and acknowledge his power.

I should not know how to answer your last letter on the passion of love with other words that seem to me more fitting than with this sonnet, from which you can see how much effort that little thief Love has spent in order to chain me; and these chains that he has put on me are so strong that I wholly despair of my liberty. I cannot think of any way in which I can unchain myself; and even if chance or some twist in human affairs should open to me some way for getting out of them, perchance I should not wish to take it; so much now sweet, now light, now heavy do I find those chains, and they make a mixture of such a sort that I judge I cannot live contented without this kind of life. And because I know how much such thoughts and news about such a life delight you, I regret that you are not here to laugh, now at my complaints, now at my laughter; and all that pleasure you might have, our Donato carries away, who together with the woman of whom I earlier wrote, are my only ports and havens for my boat, which in the unceasing storm long has been without rudder and without sails. And it is not two evenings ago that it happened that I could say, like Phoebus to Daphne:

O Nymph of Peneus, I pray, await me; I do not pursue as an enemy; Nymph, await. So the lamb from the wolf, so the deer from the lion, so the doves with trembling wing flee from the eagle, each one from his enemies.[1]

And just as to Phoebus these verses profited little, so to me the same words with her who was fleeing were of no moment, of no force.

Anybody who saw our letters, honored friend, and saw their diversity, would wonder greatly, because he would suppose now that we were grave men, wholly concerned

[1] Ovid, *Metamorphoses* 1.504-507.

with important matters, and that into our breasts no thought could fall that did not have in itself honor and greatness. But then, turning the page, he would judge that we, the very same persons, were lightminded, inconstant, lascivious, concerned with empty things. And this way of proceeding, if to some it may appear censurable, to me seems praiseworthy, because we are imitating Nature, who is variable; and he who imitates her cannot be blamed. And though we have been accustomed to this variety over many letters, I wish to practise it this time in one, as you will see, if you will read the other page. Now spit.

Your Pagolo has been here with the Magnificent,[2] and in the course of his discussions with me on his hopes, he said His Lordship has promised to make him governor of one of those cities of which he now is taking the sovereignty. And having heard, not from Pagolo but by common report, that he is to become lord of Parma, Piacenza, Modena, and Reggio, it seems to me that this dominion is good and strong, and such that under any conditions he can hold it, if in the beginning it be well governed. And if he is going to govern it well, he needs to understand well the nature of the subject. These new states, taken by a new ruler, offer, if they are to be kept, countless difficulties. And if there is difficulty in keeping those that are used to being all in one body, as, for instance, the dukedom of Ferrara, much more difficulty is found in keeping those that are newly made up of different members, as will be this of Lord Giuliano, because one part of it is a member of Milan, another of Ferrara. Therefore, he who becomes prince ought to consider making them into a single body and accustoming them to recognize one ruler as soon as possible. This can be done in two ways, either by living there in person, or by setting up a deputy there who will rule

[2] Giuliano de' Medici, Duke of Nemours, for whom his brother, Pope Leo X, was preparing a principality in northern Italy.

them all; so that those subjects, though of different cities and divided among various opinions, may look to one only and regard him as prince. And if his Lordship, wishing to remain for the present in Rome, should put there one who knew well the nature of things and the conditions of the places, he would lay a strong foundation for his new state. But if he puts into every city its own head, and His Lordship does not live there, that state will always be disunited, without reputation for him, and without bringing the prince respect or fear. Duke Valentino,[3] whose works I should always imitate if I were a new prince, realizing this necessity, made Messer Rimirro President in Romagna; that decision made those peoples united, fearful of his authority, fond of his power, and trustful in it; and all the love they felt for him, which was great, considering his newness, resulted from this decision. I believe this thing can easily be demonstrated, because it is true; and if it should happen to your Pagolo, this would be a step in making him known not merely to the Magnificent but to all Italy; and with honor and profit to His Lordship, he could give reputation to himself, to you, and to your family. I spoke of it with him; it pleased him, and he will consider making use of it. I have thought it well to write about it, so that you will know our discussions and, wherever it is necessary, can pave the way to this thing.

And in the proud rascal's fall, he nevertheless did not forget Mahomet.[4]

Our Donato sends his regards.
31 January 1514.

Niccolò Machiavelli, in Florence.

[3] Cesare Borgia. See *The Prince,* chap. 7, for his management of the territory secured for him by his father, Pope Alexander VI.
[4] Luigi Pulci, *Morgante* 1.303.

18 August 1515, Florence

To Giovanni Vernacci, in Pera

[This and the two following letters are addressed to Machiavelli's nephew.]

[Niccolò's affection]

Dearest Giovanni:

If I have not written to you in the past, I do not want you to blame either me or others, but only the times, which have been of such a sort that they have made me forget myself. Not, however, on that account have I really forgotten you, because I shall always look upon you as a son, and I and my affairs will be always at your disposal. Try to keep healthy and to do good, because from your good there can come nothing but good to whoever wishes you well.

18 August 1515.

Niccolò Machiavelli, in Florence.

No. 161

19 November 1515, Florence

To Giovanni Vernacci, in Pera

[Hopes for prosperity]

Dearest Giovanni:

I have written to you twice during the last four months, and I am sorry that you have not received my letters;

I fear that you think I do not write through being unmindful of you. This is not at all true; Fortune has left me only relatives and friends, and I make capital of them, and especially of those who are closest to me, as you are, from whom I hope, when Fortune brings you to some honorable position, that you will render to my children a return for my doings for you. Keep well.

From Florence, 19 November 1515.

Niccolò Machiavelli, in Florence.

No. 162

15 February 1516, Florence
To Giovanni Vernacci, in Pera

[Waiting for Fortune]

Dearest Giovanni:

Everytime you write to tell me that you have not received my letters, you stab me with a knife, because in the past year I have written to you six times, and given the letters to Marietta to be sent to Alberto. She says she has sent them; you say you have not received them, at which I am vexed. So the last I wrote to you two months ago I sent by Bartolomeo Federighi, who told me he gave it to somebody who was going there. I have learned through your other letter of your hardships. I thank God that they have lessened to such an extent that you are left alive and do not need to be sad any more. And if the death of those has taken from you some opportunities, your having behaved well ought to restore them to you; so do not lose your courage, and be in good spirits.

As for me, I have become useless to myself, to my relatives, and to my friends, because such has been the decision of my sad fate. And I can say nothing better than that there has been left me no other good than health for myself and all my family. I continue to wait in order to be in time to take Good Fortune when she comes, and if she does not come, to have patience. And whatever may happen to me, I shall always keep you in that place where I have had you up to now. I am yours. Christ watch over you!

15 February 1515.

Niccolò Machiavelli, in Florence.

No. 163

10 October 1516, Livorno[2]
To the Magnificent Paolo Vettori, Most Worthy Captain of the Papal Triremes

[Fever and bleeding]

Magnificent Sir:

We arrived here in Livorno today at four o'clock. This we inform you of by Antonio your servant, that you may know of our situation, and if before your[1] arrival here anything occurs to you that we can do, you can let us know about it. Of the galleys of the Bashaw nothing is heard. We have brought your Vincenzio here, with a double tertian ague; and though he has lost a pound of blood from the nose, nonetheless the fevers do not stop. If they grow a little lighter, I believe it would be well to put him in a basket carriage while the nights are less severe, and bring

[1] The texts require *our*.

him there. If you have to defer coming here, advise us of what is wanted by Your Lordship, to whom all send their warm regards.

10 October 1516.

Niccolò Machiavelli, in Livorno.[2]

No. 164

8 June 1517, Sant'Andrea in Percussina
To Giovanni Vernacci, in Pera

[Family news]

Dearest Giovanni:

As at other times I have written to you, I do not want you to wonder if I do not write or if I am slow in answering; the reason is not that I have forgotten you and that I do not esteem you as I once did, because I esteem you more; men are esteemed according to their ability, and since you have proved that you are a good and able man, I must needs love you more than I did and altogether take pride in you, since I brought you up, and since my house is the beginning of that good which you have and which you are going to have. But since I am reduced to living on my farm by the adversities that I have had and now have, I go sometimes a month without thinking about myself; so if I neglect answering you, it is not strange. I have received all your letters, and am pleased to learn that you have done and are doing well, and I can have no greater pleasure than this. And when you are through and return,

<hr>

[2] This visit to Livorno is passed over in silence by Machiavelli's most voluminous biographers, Villari and Tommasini.

my house, even though poor and wretched, will be always at your service, as it has been in the past.

Bernardo and Lodovico[1] are becoming men and I hope on your return to get employment for one of them through your means.

Marietta and all the family are well. And Marietta wishes you would bring her on your return a piece of light-brown camlet and big and little needles from Damascus. And she says that they *must* shine, for those you sent the other time were not very good. Christ watch over you.
8 June 1517.

Niccolò Machiavelli, on his farm.

No. 166

17 December 1517, Florence
To Lodovico Alamanni, at Rome

[Donato del Corno's affairs; *Orlando Furioso*]

My honored Lodovico:

I know that I do not need to take much trouble to show you how much I love Donato del Corno, and how much I desire to do anything that will bring him pleasure. Hence I know that you will not wonder if I make you some trouble for love of him, which I shall do so much the more without hesitation so far as I believe you can do it, and also as the case is just and in a sense charitable. The said Donato, after the Medici lords had been back in Florence about a month, partly on account of his obligations to the Lord Giuliano, partly on account of his good nature, without

---

[1] Niccolò's older sons.

ing asked, took Lord Giuliano five hundred ducats of ld, and told him to use it and return it when convenient.[1] Since then five years have passed, and, in spite of the great good fortune of the said lords, he has not been repaid; and being at present in some need, and knowing also that in recent days similar creditors have had their loans repaid, he has taken courage to ask for it, and has written about it to Domenico Buoninsegni, and sent him the copy of the receipt he has in Giuliano's hand. But because with such a man as Domenico, through the great number of his duties, such errands are likely to die, unless they have on their side some special influence, I have decided, in order that this one may live, to take courage to write about it, begging you will not think it an annoyance to speak about it to Domenico, and also to inquire about the way in which such money can be made ready. I hope it will not trouble you for love of me to deal with this business among your others, because, besides being merciful and just, it will not be without profit to you, and I beg you to answer with a line about it.

I have just read *Orlando Furioso* by Ariosto, and truly the poem is fine throughout, and in many places is wonderful. If he is there, give him my regards, and tell him I am only sorry that, having spoken of so many poets, he has left me out like a dog, and has done to me in his *Orlando* what I shall not do to him in my *Ass*.[2]

I know that there you are all day in the company of the Most Reverend de' Salviati, Filippo Nerli, Cosimo Rucellai, Cristofano Carnesecchi, and sometimes Anton Francesco degli Albizzi, and you give yourself to having a good time and remember little of us here, poor unfortunates dead

[1] For this loan to Giuliano de'Medici, Duke of Nemours, see the Letter of 19 December 1513, above.

[2] Machiavelli's unfinished poem commonly called *L'Asino d'Oro*, [*The Golden Ass*]. Tommasini (*Vita di Machiavelli* 2.319, n. 3) says, correctly I believe, that the proper title is merely, as in this letter, *L'Asino*, *The Ass*.

with cold and sleep. Yet, in order to seem alive, we meet sometimes, Zanobi Buondelmonti, Amerigo Morelli, Batista della Palla, and I, and we talk of that journey to France with so much vividness that it seems to us we are on the road, so that of the pleasures we would have there we have already used up half. To be able to do it with better order, we plan to make a little model of it, and to go on this last Thursday of Carnival as far as Venice, but we are in doubt whether we should get an early start and journey from there, or if we should wait until our return and go by the straight road. I wish at any rate you would consult with Cosimo and write us what is best to do. I am at your disposal. May Christ watch over you.

Give my regards to Messer Piero Ardinghelli, because I forgot to ask you to. Again farewell all.

17 December 1517.

Of the friendship and humanity of your Excellence

The servant
Niccolò Machiavelli.

No. 167

5 January 1518, Florence
To Giovanni Vernacci, in Pera

[Three more letters to Niccolò's nephew in the Levant.]

[Marriage advised]

Dearest Giovanni:

I am astonished when you say in your last letter that you have not had mine, because four months ago I wrote to you and had letters to you written by Lodovico and Bernardo, who asked you I do not know what absurdities; and the letters were given to Alberto Canigiani. As I said to you in that, if you had had it, you would not need to wonder if I have written to you seldom, because since you left I have had countless troubles, and of such a sort that they have brought me to a place where I can do little good to others and less to myself. Yet nevertheless, as I told you in that letter, my house and what remains to me are at your service, because aside from my own children, there is no man that I think so much of as I do of you. I believe your affairs have much improved in the position you have made for yourself there; and if they are in the shape I have heard, I should advise you to marry, and to marry a woman through whom you will strengthen your connection with me; and who is beautiful and has a good dower, and is of excellent standing. So I should be glad if, having to remain out there, either you would write to me or would have Alberto Canigiani tell me what your opinion is; and if you intend to take one, inform me in some way about your condition.

We are all in good health and send our regards to you. May Christ watch over you.

5 January 1517.

Niccolò Machiavelli, in Florence.

No. 168

25 January 1518, Florence
To Giovanni Vernacci, in Pera

[More on marriage]

Dearest Giovanni:

Perhaps twenty days ago I wrote you two letters with the same contents, and gave them to two persons so that you would have at least one of them. Since then I have received yours dated the fourth of November. And I am grieved to the heart that you have not had my letters, because six months ago I wrote to you and had a letter written by each of my sons, and in order that you may have one of them, I shall also make a copy of this.

As in many of my letters I have said to you, Chance, since you left, has done the worst for me that she can, so that I am brought down to a condition such that I can do little good to myself and less to others. And if I am careless in answering you, I have become so in other things; yet, while I am I, I and my house are at your disposal, as they have been always.

Many thanks for the caviar. And Marietta says that on your return you may bring her a piece of light-brown camlet.

By my other letter I wrote to you that when your affairs were in better shape, in the way I hear of and am convinced of, I should encourage you to take a wife, and if you decide to do so, there are at present some things at hand such that you would not be able to do better; so that I should be glad if in this matter you would give me some answer.

We are all in good health, and I am yours.
25 January 1517.

Your Niccolò Machiavelli, in Florence.

No. 169

15 April 1520, Florence
To Giovanni Vernacci, in Pera

[Legal troubles in Florence]

In the name of God.

Dearest Giovanni:

Since I wrote to you about the death of Alberto Canigiani, I have not had any letters from you, and also I have not written because I expected your return every hour; seeing that you have not returned, I am moved to write these few lines to do my duty by you, seeing how your things are going to ruin here. You know that Piero Venturi filed a complaint against you by which you were compelled to remit his balance, so that you suffered damage from it of sixty florins, as I am told by Piero Corsali. Besides this, there is likelihood of complaints being filed against you by Giovan Luigi Arrighetti, Giorgio Bartoli, and many others, who all have judgments against you, through there not being here anybody who can answer them or knows how to. I for my part am of no use there, because I should do you harm and not good, on account of the conditions in which I find myself. Your uncles and your father's cousins have not been willing to speak, if nothing else, to one of the six, and of friends you have nobody here who has been willing to take this trouble; so that if you do not return, you will lose property and honor. Piero Corsali has made excuses to me and tells me he has written to you. By all means, my Giovanni, consider well your course carefully, because if you stay a year more out there, you will lose everything here and will remain the prey of those who have committed you. I write this to do my duty, and so that you cannot say that it has not been written to you. May Christ watch over you.

Your Niccolò Machiavelli, in Florence.

No. 175

About 8 November 1520 (undated), Florence
To Francesco del Nero

[The contract for writing the *History of Florence*][1]
To his honored brother-in-law, Francesco del Nero

Honored Sir:
The substance of the contract will be this:

He is to be hired for _____ years with an annual salary of _____, with the obligation that he must and will be held to write the annals or history of the things done by the state and city of Florence, beginning with the date that seems to him suitable, and in that language—whether Latin or Tuscan—that seems to him best.

Niccolò Machiavelli

No. 179

17 May 1521, Carpi
To his Magnificent Master Francesco Guicciardini, J.U.D., Governor of Mantua and Reggio, most worthy and especially to be honored.

[Machiavelli was sent to Carpi, on the occasion of the meeting of the *Capitolo* or General Assembly of the Franciscan order, to transact business for the Medici govern-

[1] Officially this employment came from the University of Pisa, of which Francesco del Nero was commissioner. It was approved by Giulio de'Medici, Pope Clement VII.

ment of Florence. The officers of the Florentine Art of Wool also requested him to secure for them a Lenten preacher.]

[A preacher for Florence; the comedy of business]

Magnificent Sir, Ruler to be Most Respected:

I was on the privy-seat when your messenger came, and just then I was thinking of the absurdities of this world; I was giving all my attention to imagining for myself a preacher to my taste for the place at Florence, and he would be just what would please me, because in this I intend to be obstinate as in my other opinions. And because I never failed that city by not benefiting her when I could, if not with deeds, with words, if not with words, with gestures, I do not intend to fail her this time either. It is true that I know I am opposed, as in many other things, to the opinion of the citizens there: they would like a preacher who would show them the road to Paradise, and I should like to find one who would teach them the way to go to the house of the Devil; they would like, besides, that he should be a man prudent, blameless, and true; and I should like to find one crazier than Ponzo, more crafty than Fra Girolamo, more of a hypocrite than Frate Alberto,[1] because it would seem to me a fine thing, and worthy of the goodness of these times, that all we have experienced in many friars should be experienced in one, because I believe the true way of going to Paradise would be to learn the road to Hell in order to avoid it. Seeing, besides this, how much credit a bad man has who conceals himself under the cloak of religion, I can easily conjecture how much of it a good man would have who in truth and not in pretense continued to tread muddy places like St. Francis. So since my fancy seemed to me good, I have planned to

[1] Ponzo is unknown; Fra Girolamo is Savonarola; Frate Alberto is from the *Decameron* 4.2.

choose Rovaio, and I believe that if he is like his brothers and sisters, he will be just right. I should be glad if, next time you write, you will give me your opinion.

I continue in idleness here because I cannot carry out my commission until the general and the assessors are chosen, and I keep ruminating on how I can sow so much discord among them that either here or elsewhere they may start hitting each other with their sandals; and if I do not lose my wits, I believe I am going to succeed; and I believe that the advice and help of Your Lordship would assist greatly. So if you would come as far as here, as a pleasure jaunt, it would not be a bad thing, or at least by writing suggest some master strokes; because if you once every day would send me a servant just for this purpose, as you have today, you would do several good things: for one, you would give me light on some things quite to my purpose; for another, you would make me more esteemed by those in the house, seeing the messages come thick. And I can tell you that on the arrival of this arbalester with the letter, and making a bow down to the earth, and with his saying that he was sent specially and in haste, everybody rose up with so many signs of respect and such a noise that everything was turned upsidedown, and I was asked by several about the news; and I, that its reputation might grow, said that the Emperor was expected at Trent, and that the Swiss had summoned new diets, and that the King of France wanted to go in person to speak with that king, but that his councilors advised him against it; so that they all stood with open mouths and with their caps in their hands; and while I write I have a circle of them around me, and seeing me write at length they are astonished, and look on me as inspired; and I, to make them wonder more, sometimes hold my pen still and swell up, and then they slaver at the mouth; but if they could see what I am writing, they would marvel at it more. Your Lordship knows that these friars say that when one is confirmed in grace, the Devil has no more power to tempt him. So I have no more fear that these friars will make me a hypocrite, because I believe I am very well confirmed.

As to the lies of the Carpigiani, I should like a contest in that matter with all of them, because quite a while ago I trained myself in such a way that I do not need Francesco Martelli for a servant: for a long time I have not said what I believed, nor do I ever believe what I say, and if indeed sometimes I do happen to tell the truth, I hide it among so many lies that it is hard to find.

To that governor I did not speak, because having found lodgings, it seemed to me that to speak to him was useless. It is true that this morning in church I stared at him a bit, while he was standing to look at some paintings. His outside seemed to me well made, and I can believe that the whole corresponds to the part, and that he is what he seems, and that Telda is not crazy,[2] so that if I had had your letter with me, I should have made an attempt at drawing a bucketful out of him. Still not a thing has happened, and I expect tomorrow some advice from you on my affairs, and that you will send one of the same arbalesters, and that he will hurry and get here all sweaty, so that the household will be amazed; for by so doing you will bring me honor, and at the same time your arbalesters will get a little exercise, which for the horses on these spring days is very wholesome.

I might write you some other things now, if I were willing to weary my fancy, but I wish for tomorrow to keep it as fresh as I can. I send my regards to Your Lordship, and may you ever prosper as you desire.

In Carpi, 17 May 1521.

> Your faithful Niccolò Machiavelli,
> Ambassador to the Minor Friars.

[2] Unknown.

No. 182

18 May 1521, Carpi
To Francesco Guicciardini, at Modena

[See the head-note of the preceding letter.]

[The comedy of the friars; Rovaio as preacher]

I can tell you that the smoke of it has gone up to the sky, because between the panting of the carrier and the great bundle of letters, there is not a man in this house and in this neighborhood who is not overcome with fear; and in order not to seem ungrateful to Messer Gismondo, I showed him those sections about the Swiss and the King. He thought it a great thing. I spoke to him of the sickness of Caesar and of the states he wished to buy in France in such a way that it made him drool. But I believe that with all this he fears being made to act, because he keeps considering, and does not see why it is necessary to write such long bibles in these deserts of Arabia, where there is no one except friars; and I do not think I appear to him that unusual man of whom you have written to him, because I remain here in the house, or I sleep or I read or I keep quiet; so that I believe he concludes that you wish to play a joke on both me and him. Still he keeps testing, and I reply to him in a few words and badly put together, and rely on the flood that is to come, or on the Turk who is going to cross over,[1] and if it would be a good thing to carry on a Crusade in these days, and similar stories for tavern benches; so that I believe it seems to him a thousand

---

[1] A common and comic source of fear at the time. See the Introduction, section 8, above.

years until he can talk with you yourself, in order to have things explained better, and to raise questions with you, who have put this grease on his hands,[2] because I disturb his house and keep him obligated here. Yet I believe he is very sure that the play can last but a short time, and therefore he continues putting a good face on it and making the meals good; and I gobble them up like six dogs and three wolves, and say when I dine: "This morning I gain two *giulii*." And when I have supper: "This evening I gain four of them." Yet all the same I am under obligation to you and to him, and if he ever comes to Florence I will make it up to him, and you meanwhile will give him words.

This traitor Rovaio gets himself urged, and then finds fault, and says he fears he cannot come, because he does not know what methods he could then use in preaching, and he fears to go into the galley as though he were Pope Angelico;[3] and he says that he is not now honored in Florentine affairs, for they made a law when he preached there the other time that whores would have to appear in Florence with yellow veils, and that he has a letter from his sister that they appear as they please, and that they flourish their tails more than ever; and he was very sorry about this thing. Still I kept on consoling him, saying that he should not be astonished at it, that it was the custom of great cities not to stand firm long in a decision, and to do today a thing and tomorrow to undo it; and I brought up Rome and Athens, so that he was entirely consoled and almost promised me. By my next you will learn the rest.

This morning these friars here have elected their Minister General, who is Soncino; he was first a man, secondly a friar, humane and good. This evening I must appear before their paternities, and tomorrow I believe I shall be entirely

---

[2] This profit procured for him. Ironical.

[3] Pope Angelico, the angelic pope, is the ideally good pontiff of popular verse. Machiavelli suggests that he would be sent to the galley (to prison) because opposed to the ambitions of influential clerics.

finished, so that every hour seems to me a thousand, and I shall then stay one day with Your Lordship, who I hope will live and reign for ages of ages.

18 May 1521

Niccolò Machiavelli
Ambassador of the Florentine State
to the Minor Friars

No. 183

19 May 1521, Carpi
To Francesco Guicciardini

[See the head-note of Letter no. 179.]

[More difficulty about the preacher; the friars]

Catso! One needs to manage cleverly in dealing with that fellow, because he is as tricky as thirty thousand devils. I believe he's aware you are making game of him, because when the messenger came, he said: "Whew! this must be some big affair; the messengers come fast." Then, after reading your letter, he said: "I believe the governor is making fools of me and you." I acted Albanese, Messere,[1] and said that I left certain business at Florence in a matter that pertained to you and me, and I had asked that you would keep me informed when you learned from there anything about it, and that this was the chief cause for the writing; so my arse goes "Lappe, Lappe,"[2] because I am afraid all the time he will make a clean sweep and send

---

[1] He tried not to give a direct reply. Cf. the end of Burchiello's *Sonnet* 1.73 (*La violente casa*).

[2] Cf. Pulci, *Morgante* 24.125. A comic way of referring to noises in the bowels produced by fear. Gluttony is indicated by *lappe, lappe* in the throat (*Malmantile Racquistato* 5.62).

me back to the inn; hence I beg that tomorrow you will take a holiday, so that this sport will not become injurious, though the good I have received cannot be taken from my body; splendid food, glorious beds, and such things, in which I have for three days now been rejuvenated.

This morning I have made a beginning on the case of the division;[3] today I have to be attending to it; tomorrow I believe I shall finish it.

As to the preacher, I do not expect to get any honor from it, because this fellow holds off; the father in charge says he is promised to others, so I believe I shall go back in disgrace; and I don't like it at all, because I don't know how to appear before Francesco Vettori and Filippo Strozzi, who wrote about it to me especially, begging me to do everything, in order that this Lent they could feed on spiritual food that would do them good. And they will be sure to say that in everything I serve them the same way, because this winter just past, when I was with them one Saturday evening at the villa of Giovan Francesco Ridolfi, they gave me the duty of getting the priest for the mass of next morning; and then the thing went in such a way that that blessed priest arrived after they had dined, so everything there was upside down, and I got the blame for it. Now if in this second commission I rebottle the wine on the dregs, imagine what an angry face they will turn on me. Yet I am reckoning that you will write them two lines and excuse me in this affair as well as you can.

About the *History* and the state of the wooden sandals, I do not believe I have lost anything by coming here, because I have learned many institutions and such of their regulations as are good; for I believe I can make use of it for various purposes, especially in comparisons, because where I need to speak of silence I can say: "They were

[3] Machiavelli's mission was to get the Minor Friars to divide their province so that Tuscany would be separately administered.

204

keeping more quiet than the brothers when they eat," and so I can make use of many other things I have learned from this bit of experience.

19 May 1521

Your Niccolò Machiavelli.

No. 185

26 September 1523, Sant'Andrea in Percussina
To Francesco del Nero, in Florence

[Some business matters]

Honored brother-in-law:

Patience with the troubles I make you. The churches are interdicted, as you will see by the enclosed; and on account of the study, I beg you to send me by Bologna the release, which I am sending to you by messenger; otherwise I shall have that chimney relaid. And I shall give your regards to the fowls. I am yours.

26 September 1523.

Niccolò Machiavelli, on his farm.

No. 186

30 August 1524, Sant'Andrea in Percussina
To Francesco Guicciardini

[At work on the *History of Florence*]

[The beginning is lacking] I have been staying and now stay on my farm to write the *History*, and I would pay ten *soldi*—but no more—to have you by my side so that I could show you where I am, because, having come to certain particulars, I need to learn from you if I give too much offense either by raising or by lowering these things.[1] But I shall keep on taking counsel with myself and shall try to act in such a way that, since I tell the truth, nobody will be able to complain.

30 August 1524.

Your Niccolò Machiavelli.

[1] A reference to what he might say about the ancestors of the Medici and of other Florentines as well. On this subject in the Preface to the *History of Florence*, he suggests that if ancestors are made famous the quality of their actions matters little.

No. 192

3 August 1525, Florence
To Francesco Guicciardini

[Tuscan farms]

Mr. President:

I have put off writing until today, because before today I could not go to see the property of Colombaia, so I trust Your Lordship will excuse me for this delay.

I shall begin everything from Finochieto.[1] And I must tell you as the first thing this: for three miles around one sees nothing pleasing; stony Arabia is not different. The house cannot be called bad, but I would never call it good, because it is without those conveniences that are sought for; the rooms are small, the windows are high; a dungeon is not made differently. It has in front a rough meadow; all

[1] *Finochieto*, the name of the farm, is the diminutive of *finocchio* (fennel). This was proverbially the last thing to come on the dining table. See Pulci, *Morgante* 18.198; 19.62; 25.291. Machiavelli is amused at his reversal of the normal order.

the exits go off downward, except one that has level ground for perhaps 200 feet; and with all this it is buried among the mountains in such a way that the longest view does not exceed half a mile. As to the farms, what they pay Your Lordship knows, but they are in danger of paying every year less; because they have many fields that the water washes in such a way that if great diligence is not used there to hold the soil with ditches, in a short time there will be nothing there but the bones; this demands the master, and you are too far away. I hear that the Bartolini have made a purchase in that region and that they lack a guest-house. If you could get rid of it to them, I should encourage you to do so, because it is a good thing for them and ought to save you loss. If they do not come into your hands, whether you wish to hold it or to sell it, I would encourage you to spend 100 ducats, with which you could complete work on the meadow, encircle with vines almost all of the hill where the house is placed, and make eight or ten ditches in those fields that are between your house and that of your first farm, which fields are called la Chiusa. In these ditches I would put winter fruits and figs; I would make a fountain at a fine spring that is in the middle of those fields at the foot of some rows of vines, which is the only fine thing there. This improvement will serve you for one of two things: the first is that, if you decide to sell, anybody who comes to see it sees something that pleases him, and perhaps will then wish to talk about buying; for if you keep it as it is, and the Bartolini do not buy it, I do not believe you will ever sell it, except to someone who does not come to see it, like yourself. If you decide to keep it, the said improvements will serve to get you more vines, which are good, and will keep you from dying of sorrow when you go to see it. So enough about Finochieto.

Of Colombaia, I confirm, so far as I can observe with the eye, all that Jacopo has written you and Girolamo has said.

The farm lies well, has its roads and ditches around the villa,[2] and faces between south and east. The fields seem good, because all the fruit trees, old and young, have much vigor and life in them. It has all conveniences of church, of butcher, of road, of post, that a farm near Florence can have. It has a great many fruit trees, and nevertheless there is space to double them. The house is made like this: you enter a court that is on each side about 40 feet; it has in front, opposite the gate, a loggia with a balcony above, and it is as long as the size of the court and about 27 feet broad. This loggia has on the right hand of him who looks toward it a room with an anteroom; and on the left hand a hall, with room and anteroom; all these rooms with the loggia are habitable and not undignified; it has in this court a kitchen, a stable, a vatroom and another little court for poultry and for cleaning the house. It has underneath two wine cellars of excellent design; it has many rooms above, of which there are three that for ten ducats could be prepared for lodging men of some rank. The roofs are neither bad nor good. In short, I assure you of this, that with an expense of 150 ducats you could live comfortably, pleasantly, and not at all without dignity. These 150 ducats you would need to spend in remaking doors, paving courts, remaking some parapets, replacing a beam, repairing a stair, remaking the eaves of the roof, renovating and rearranging a kitchen, and similar small matters that give appearance and cheerfulness to a house; and so with this expense you can live as well as you could even by entering into a great sea.[3]

As to the rents, I have not yet examined them to suit me, since a man to whom I wished to speak was not there. In another letter I shall give Your Lordship a detailed account.

[2] The texts print *valla*. I have ventured the emendation of *villa*.
[3] Great expenses.

This morning I received yours, informing me that I am in high favor with the Maliscotta; in that I take more pleasure than in anything I have in this world. I shall be pleased to have you give her my regards.

On the affairs of the kings, the emperors, and the popes, I have nothing to write; perhaps for another letter I shall have something, and I shall write.

I pray Your Lordship to tell Madonna V. that I have given her greetings to all her friends, men and women, and especially to Averardo; all of whom send regards to Your Lordship and to her. And to Your Lordship I send numberless regards and offers of service.

3 August 1525

Your Niccolò Machiavelli, in Florence

No. 196

17 August 1525, Florence
To Francesco Guicciardini

[*Mandragola;* pills for stomach and head;
a marriage negotiation]

Mr. President:

Yesterday I had yours of the twelfth, and in reply will tell you that Capponi returned, and this trouble of asking him has been taken on by Your Jacopo; so, as you say, I believe he will be sufficiently understood. You can at least make them an offer, to let them see that you wish it, if they do not depart from what is honorable. Girolamo and I think that you cannot offer less than 3000 ducats; yet for this you can give him such a commission as you like.

It pleases me that *Messer Nicia*[1] pleases you, and if you have it presented in this Carnival, we will come to help you. I thank you for the commendations given and beseech you to continue them.

These overseers of the affairs of the Levant intend to send me to Venice for the recovery of some lost funds. If I go, I shall leave within three days, and in returning shall come where you are to spend an evening with Your Lordship and to see my friends.

I send you twenty-five pills made four days ago in your name, and the recipe will be written at the end of this. I tell you that they have restored me. Begin by taking one of them after supper; if that causes a movement, do not take any more of them; if it does not cause a movement, two or three, and at most five; but I never took more than two, and in a week only once, and when I feel myself heavy in the stomach or the head.

Two days ago I spoke on that affair with our friend, and said that if I was going too far into his affairs of importance, he should excuse me for it, since he was the one who had given me courage, and briefly I asked him his intention about giving a wife to his son. He answered me, after some ceremonies, that he thought things had come to such a pass that young men nowadays think it disgraceful not to have an extraordinary dower, and he did not believe it in his power to bring his son to an ordinary one. Then having stood for a little while considering: "I believe I know for what reason you speak to me, because I know where you have been, and this discussion has been brought before me by other means." To which I answered that I did not know whether he guessed well or not, but that the truth was that between you and me there had never been any such discussion, which I demonstrated to him with all sorts of effective words; and if I was acting,

[1] An alternative title for Machiavelli's comedy now called *Mandragola*.

I was acting for myself and because of the good I wished to him and to me; and here I took the mask off from him and from you, and from your situation, and from the nature of present and future times, and said so many things that I made him uncertain; so at last he admitted that if the Magnificent should decide to take as his wife a Florentine, he would be badly advised if he did not take her from your house. Hence I said I did not see how you, by a man like him who had sense, could be swapped for some other citizen for two or three thousand ducats more; moreover, since you have no sons and your wife has ceased bearing, chance might make the dower turn out larger than that of some one else he might take, from whom he could not get anything further than the dower. And because in the course of this discussion we walked to the Servi, I stopped at the door and said to him: "I wish to speak this last word to you in a place to be remembered, so that you will recall it. May God grant that you be not obliged to repent of it, and may your son not be forced to feel that he has little obligation to you." So he said: "In God's name, this is the first time we have talked about it; we must speak of it every day." To which I said that I was not ever again going to say a single thing about it, because it was enough for me to have paid my debt. In this way I have managed my spear, for I could not conceal what I was certain he was going to find out. I am now prepared to wait for him and not to miss any opportunity, and with discussions general and particular to hammer on this point.

But let us turn to the recipe for the pills.

Recipe

Hepatic Aloes	Dram.	1½	
Germander	"	1	—
Saffron	"	—	½

Selected Myrrh	"	—	½
Betony	"	—	½
Pimpernel	"	—	½
Armenian Bole	"	—	½

Niccolò Machiavelli, in Florence
17 August 1525

No. 198

September 1525, Florence
To Francesco Guicciardini

[Some phrases in Machiavelli's comedy, *Mandragola*]

Mr. President:

Since immediately on arriving I went to my farm, and found my Bernardo sick with a double tertian, I have not written to you. But on returning this morning from the farm to speak with the doctor, I found one from Your Lordship of the thirteenth, through which I see into what distress of mind you have been brought by the foolishness of *Messer Nicia* and the ignorance of those fellows. And though I believe your doubts are many, nevertheless since you make plain that you wish the explanation of not more than two, I shall try to satisfy you.

To take to stones for ovens does not mean anything other than to do something fit for mad men, and therefore that character of mine says that if all were like Messer Nicia, "We would take to stones for ovens," that is, we would all do things fit for mad men, and this is enough for the first doubt.[1]

[1] *Mandragola* 2.4.

As to the toad and the harrow,[2] this has indeed need for greater consideration. And truly I have thumbed through many books, like Fra Timoteo, to find the source of this harrow, and at last I have found in Burchiello a text that supports me, where in one of his sonnets he says:

Fearing that the sovereignty would pass away,
There was sent as Ambassador a kettle of thread,
The tongs and the shovel were pursued,
So that he found himself thereby poorer by four ropes,
But the harrow of Fiesole drew there . . .

This sonnet seems to me full of mystery; and I believe he who considers it well may continue to stir up our times. There is only this difference, that if now any one sends a kettle of thread, that thread is changed into macaroni, so that it seems to me that all times return and that we are always the same people. The harrow is a construction of square wood that has certain teeth, and our farmers use it when they wish to prepare the fields for seeds, in order to plant them. Burchiello brings forward the harrow of Fiesole as the most ancient in Tuscany, because the Fiesolani, as Titus Livius says in his second decade,[3] were the first to invent this instrument. And one day when a farmer was leveling his field, a toad that was not used to seeing such great labor, while she wondered and gaped to see what was up there, was run over by the harrow, which scratched her back in such a way that she put her paw there more than twice. Hence, as the harrow passed over her, when the toad felt herself hit hard, she said to him: "Don't come back." This word gave rise to the proverb that runs, when one wishes a person will not return, "As the toad said to the harrow." This is all I have found of value, and if Your Lordship has any uncertainty, let me know.

[2] *Mandragola* 3.6.
[3] A jocose touch; the second decade of Livy is not extant.

While you are active there, we here also do not sleep, because Lodovico Alamanni and I sup these evenings with la Barbera and talk of the comedy, so that she offers to come with her singers to furnish the chorus between the acts; and I offer myself to make the songs in harmony with the acts, and Lodovico offers to give lodging there in the house of the Buosi to her and her singers. So you see that we are attending to business, in order that this festival may have all its fitting parts. With my regards, etc.

Your Niccolò Machiavelli.

No. 199

November [?] 1525, Florence
To Francesco Guicciardini

[More on the marriages of Guicciardini's daughters; how to get money from princes]

Mr. President:

I never remember Your Lordship (and I remember you every hour) that I do not reflect on the way for doing something to fulfil your wish in the thing that, as I know, among the others most presses upon you; and among the many fantasies that have come to my mind, there has been one which I have determined to write, not in order to advise you but merely to open a door, through which you will know better than anyone else how to pass. Filippo Strozzi finds himself burdened with sons and daughters; and as he seeks to honor his sons, so he believes it proper to honor his daughters. He also believes, as all wise men believe, that the eldest girl should show the way to the others. He tried, among various young men, to give her to a son of Giuliano Capponi with four thousand florins of dowry, but he did not get what he wished, because Giuliano did not approve; so Filippo, despairing of doing anything good by himself, unless committed himself so with the dowry that he afterward could not keep it up, applied to the Pope for aid, and through his suggestion took up the business with Lorenzo Ridolfi, and concluded it with eight thousand florins of dowry, of which four thousand were paid by the Pope and four thousand by himself. Pagolo Vettori, wishing to make an honorable marriage, and not seeing any prospect for giving a dowry that would be enough, also applied to the Pope, and he, to please Pagolo, put there along with his influence two thousand ducats of his own.

My dear President, if you were the first who had to break this ice to travel in this direction, I should be one of those who perhaps would go slowly in advising you to try it, but having had the way already prepared for you by two men who, for qualities, merits, and every other human consideration, are not your superiors, I shall always advise that you courageously and without any hesitation do what they have done. Filippo has gained with the aid of the Pope a hundred and fifty thousand ducats, and he has not hesitated to ask the Pope to aid him in that necessity; much less do you need to hesitate who have not gained twenty thousand. Pagolo has been aided countless times and in countless ways, not with offices but with money itself, and then without hesitation has asked the Pope to aid him in that need. Much less hesitation in doing it is proper for you, who have been aided not with trouble to the Pope, but with honor and profit to him. I need not remind you of Palla Rucellai, or Bartolommeo Valori, or of a great many others who in their necessities have been aided from the Pope's purse; these examples I believe should make you bold in asking and confident of obtaining what you ask. Hence if I were in your position, I should write a letter to your agent at Rome, who would read it to the Pope, or I would write it to the Pope and have it presented to him by the agent, and to him in secret I should send a copy of it and should instruct him that he should see that he got a reply to it. I suggest that the letter should show that you have worked ten years to gain honor and profit, and that it seems to you that in both you have very well satisfied such a desire, though with very great hardships and dangers, for which you thank God first and then the blessed memory of Pope Leo and His Holiness,[1] to whom you owe the whole. It is true that you know very well that if men do ten things with honor and then fail in one, especially when that one is of some importance, it has power to blot out all the others; and therefore since you feel that in many things you have carried out the part of a man of ability, you would wish not to be lacking in anything. And having written such a preamble, I would show him what your condition is, and that you are without sons, but have four daughters, and that it is time to marry off one of them; and if you do not marry her in such a way that this act corresponds with your other achievements, you will feel that you have never done anything of value. And then you can show that to this desire of yours nothing is opposed except the wicked ways and corrupt customs of the present time, since the matter is brought to such a pass that in proportion as a young man is nobler and richer, laying aside all other considerations, he wishes a larger dower; indeed, when they do not receive dowers great beyond all reason, they think themselves disgraced. You do not know how to overcome this difficulty, because if you give three thousand florins, that will be as far as you could go, and it is so much that four daughters would require twelve thousand, which is all the profit made by

[1] Pope Clement VII.

216

your dangers and labors. Not being able to go higher, you recognize such a dower as only half of what young men demand. Hence, as the only remedy, you have plucked up courage to do what his better friends, among whom you account yourself, have done, that is, to go for support and aid to His Holiness, not believing that what he has done for others he will deny you. And there I should reveal to him the young man you have planned on, and how you know that the dower and nothing else thwarts you; and therefore it is necessary that His Holiness overcome this difficulty. And here press him and bear him down with the most effective words you know how to find, to show him how important you think the matter; and I feel sure, if it is dealt with at Rome in any reasonable way, that you will succeed. So do not fail yourself, and if time and the season permit it, I should encourage you to send your Girolamo there for this purpose, because the whole thing consists in asking boldly, and showing great discontent if you do not receive. And princes easily bend themselves to do new favors for those for whom they have done old ones, or rather they are so afraid of losing, if they refuse, the benefits of their earlier favors, that they always hasten to confer new ones, when they are asked in such a way as I hope you will ask this. You are prudent.

Morone was seized, and the dukedom of Milan is overthrown; and as he has waited for the hood,[2] all the other princes will wait for it, and there is no further recourse. Thus it is imposed from above.[3]

> I see into Alagna the fleur-de-lys entering,
> And in his vicar, etc.[4]

[2] A figure of speech, taken from the gentle falcon that waits for its hood to be put on, meaning *to submit tamely*. Morone was High Chancellor of the Dukedom of Milan.

[3] Seemingly a quotation.

[4] Dante, *Purgatorio* 20.86. I have translated Dante's text; the form usually used in editions of Machiavelli is incorrect, perhaps a misprint.

You know the verses; read the rest for yourself. Let us make for once a gay Carnival; and you prepare for Barbera a lodging among those friars we know of, and if they don't go mad, I don't want any money from it; and give my regards to Maliscotta, and let me know how far along the comedy is and when you plan to present it.

I received that addition, making a total of a hundred ducats for the *History*.[5] I am now beginning to write again, and I relieve myself by blaming the princes, who have all done everything to bring us here. Farewell.

Niccolò Machiavelli
Historian, comic writer, and tragic writer[6]

No. 200

19 December 1525, Florence
To Francesco Guicciardini

[More on the dowers for Guicciardini's daughters]

Mr. President:

I have put off answering your last until this day, both because it did not seem to me pressing and because I have not been much in Florence. Now having seen your master of the stables there and thinking I can send a letter securely, I have not put it off longer. I cannot deny that your hesitation, on whether it is good to attempt that business or not in such a way, is good and wisely presented; nonetheless I shall give you my opinion, which is that

---

[5] Machiavelli was first paid in sealed florins, depreciated nearly one-half. The ducat had not depreciated.

[6] The first two parts of this description are literal. Figuratively, Machiavelli could think of himself as a tragic writer because he dealt with the sorrows of Italy, referred to in the closing sentence of the letter.

one can make a mistake in being too prudent as much as in being too rash; indeed to be of the latter sort is often better. If Filippo and Pagolo had had these qualms, they would not have done what they wanted to, and if Pagolo does not have daughters that will lead the way to the others, Filippo has some, but he hasn't thought about them, if only he can settle the first to his taste. And I do not know if there is truth in what you say, that you will put the first in Heaven only to put the others in Hell, since this action will not put you in a worse condition with the others than you are in now with all of them; rather in a better one, because the other sons-in-law, besides having you, will have an honorable brother-in-law, and you will find some who are less avaricious and more honorable; in fact, even if you do not find them, those chances that you now find for this daughter will not fail you for the others. So then I should try the Pope in any case, and if I did not come to half sword the first time, I should speak of it to him in general terms, tell him my desire, beg him to help me, see where I find him, go ahead and draw back, according as it went. I remind you of the advice that Romeo gave to the Duke of Provence, who had four daughters, and he encouraged him to marry the first honorably, telling him that she would give the others a norm and precedent. So he married her to the king of France, and gave him half Provence as a dower. As a result, with small dowers he married the others to three other kings, as Dante says:

Four daughters he had, and each one a queen, of which thing the sole cause was Romeo, a humble man and a foreigner.[1]

I am pleased to learn the queries of these friars, which I do not wish to decide here, but there, in that place,

[1] *Paradiso* 6.133-135, modified.

and we shall go with him who will do best for us. But I can tell you, though, that if the rumor upsets them, presence sets them to fighting.

Of the things of the world I have nothing to tell you, since everybody cooled down on the Duke of Pescara's death,[2] because before his death they talked of new restrictions and similar things; but now that he is dead, each man is a little reassured, and since he seems to have time, he gives time to his enemy. And I conclude at last that on this side there is no possibility for doing, ever, anything honorable or vigorous about living or dying with justice, so much fear I observe in our citizens, and so unwilling they are to oppose him who is getting ready to swallow them up, nor do I see any exception to this; so that he who has to act after consulting with them will not do anything different than has been done up to now.

Your Niccolò Machiavelli, in Florence.

No. 202

3 January 1526, Florence
To Francesco Guicciardini

[In this double letter Machiavelli first deals with the plans for performing his comedy of *Messer Nicia,* or *Mandragola,* at Faenza, a city under Guicciardini's government.

Machiavelli then turns to the subject that engrossed his effort and fills his letters from now until the end: the

[2] The Marquis of Pescara was probably the most important general in the army of the Emperor Charles V which defeated and captured Francis I of France at the battle of Pavia in 1525. He negotiated with Morone (See Letter no. 199) as though to betray the Emperor and make himself King of Naples, but revealed the negotiations to Charles V. On 3 December 1525 he died.

progress in Italy of the armies of the Emperor Charles V. Important are the Emperor's relations with Francis I, King of France. That king, captured at the battle of Pavia, was the Emperor's prisoner from 24 February 1525 to 18 March 1526. The treaty of Madrid, signed 14 January 1526, arranged his release on conditions such as are given in the present letter. To Machiavelli, however, that release seemed so unwise that as late as 15 March he thought it unlikely. On 22 May 1526, the Treaty of Cognac against the Emperor was concluded between Pope Clement VII, Venice, Duke Francesco Sforza of Milan, and Francis I. To the alliance the French gave little assistance. The chief imperial officers were the Constable Charles of Bourbon (who had turned against King Francis I), the Marquis of Vasto, and Antonio de Leyva. Late in 1526 George Frundsberg added to the imperial forces 14,000 German soldiers. The chief officer of the allied forces opposed to them was the Duke of Urbino, who proved either unable or unwilling to make any vigorous effort against the imperial army. Pope Clement VII failed to take proper measures for defence. The imperial force moved south until on 6 May 1527 it entered Rome. The city was sacked. As secretary of the board in charge of the walls of Florence, Machiavelli labored to prepare the city for an assault. When he wrote his last letter, such attack seemed imminent, but instead of pausing, the imperial army moved directly on Rome. On 22 June 1527 Machiavelli died.]

[*Mandragola;* Charles V and Francis I]

Mr. President:

I believed that I could begin this letter of mine in reply to your last in happiness, and I have to begin it in sorrow, since your nephew is so greatly mourned by everybody, and soon after has come the death of your mother—a blow truly not expected, and deserved neither by her nor by Girolamo. Nonetheless, since God has willed it so, it must be so, and there being no defense, we must think of it as little as possible.

As to the letter from Your Lordship, I shall begin where

you do, in order to live, in the midst of such disturbances, happily; and I can say this, that I shall come no matter what, and nothing can hinder me other than sickness, from which may God protect me, and I shall come when this month is over, and at the time that you set. As to the Barbera and the singers, if some other consideration does not restrain you, I believe I can bring her for fifteen soldi to the lira. I say this because she has certain lovers who may impede it; yet, if I am diligent, they can be quieted. And that she and I have decided to come, this assures you, that we have made five new canzone suited to the comedy —and they are set to music to be sung between acts— of which I send you, enclosed with this, the words, so that Your Lordship can consider them; either all of us or I alone will bring you the music. You will need, though, if she is going to come, to send here a servant of yours with two or three animals. And this is all about the comedy.

I have always been of the opinion that if the Emperor intends to become master of affairs, he will never release the King,[1] because by keeping him he keeps all his opponents weak, so that for this reason they are giving him and will give him as much time as he wishes to organize. Thus he keeps now France and now the Pope in hope of truce, and does not break off the negotiations and does not finish them; and when he sees that the Italians are about to unite with France, he limits his discussions with France, so that France does not decide. Hence he gains, as with these tricks we see he already has gained Milan, and was on the point of gaining Ferrara; he would have succeeded if he had gone there; and if that had happened, it would have been the finish of Italy. And if I may speak of these Spanish brothers of ours, they have erred this time, for when the Duke passed through Lombardy to go there, they should have held him and made him

---

[1] Charles V will not release Francis I, captured at the battle of Pavia.

go to Spain by sea, and not have trusted him to go there by himself, because they should have known that many chances could come up (as there have), through which he would not go there.

We heard four days ago of closer relations between Italy and France, and it is credible, because, Pescara being dead, Antonio de Leyva being sick, the Duke having returned to Ferrara, the castles of Milan and Cremona still being held, the Venetians not put under obligation, and everybody clear about the ambition of the Emperor, we suppose that everybody will try to gain security, and that the chance is very good. But thereupon news comes that the Emperor and France have made an agreement, and that France yields Burgundy and takes as wife the sister of the Emperor; and he abandons four hundred thousand ducats she has of dower, and dowers her with as much; and he gives as hostages either his two younger sons or the Dauphin; and he cedes to him all the territories of Naples, of Milan, etc. Many believe in such an agreement and many do not, for the reasons given above; but I believe he has made it to hinder those closer relations mentioned above, and later he will find fault with it and break it. Now we shall wait to see what will happen.

I understand what you tell me of your business, and that you think you have time for reflection, since the times are not suitable. To this I shall answer in a few words with that sincerity which the love and reverence I bear you require. Always, as far as I recall, war has either been going on or it has been talked of. Now it is being talked of; in a short time it will be carried on; and when it is finished it will be talked of again, so that there never will be a time for thinking of anything; and to me it seems that these times are better for your business than are quiet ones, because if the Pope plans to take trouble, or fears that trouble will be made for him, he must consider that he has need, and great need, of you, and consequently must wish to please you.

Your Niccolò Machiavelli, in Florence.

No. 204

15 March 1526, Florence
To Francesco Guicciardini

[See the head-note of Letter no. 202.]

[Will Charles V release his prisoner, Francis I?;
Giovanni of the Black Bands]

Magnificent and Honorable Messer Francesco:

I have delayed writing so long that Your Lordship has got ahead of me. The cause of my delay has been that, since it seemed peace would be made, I believed you would soon be returning into Romagna, and I held back in order to speak to you by word of mouth, though I had my head full of fantasies, of which I poured out part, five or six days ago, to Filippo Strozzi. Because, writing to him about something else, I got myself started in the dance, and I debated three propositions: one, in spite of the treaty the King will not be free; two, if the King is freed, he will keep the treaty; three, he will not observe it. I did not say which of these three I believed, but I did decide that from any of these Italy would have war, and for this war I offered no preventive. Now, seeing from your letter your wish, I shall discuss with you what I was silent about with him, and so much the more willingly, since you have asked it.

If you should ask me which of these three things I believe, I cannot get away from the settled opinion I have always held, that the King is not going to be free, because everybody knows that if the King should do what he can do, he would cut off from the Emperor all the ways by which the latter can rise to the level he has planned for himself. I do not see any cause or reason strong enough to move him to let the King go. Hence, in my view, it must be that he will let him go either because his council has been bribed (something in which the French are masters), or because he sees that closer relations are certain between the Italians and the kingdom,[1] and it does not appear to him that he has time or means for breaking them up without the release of the King. He must believe, too, that the King, if released, will have to keep the terms, and the King in this matter must have been a large promiser, and shown in every way the causes of the hatred he has for the Italians, and other reasons he could bring forward to assure the Emperor of observance.

Nevertheless, all the reasons that can be brought forward do not guard the Emperor from being stupid, if the King intends to be wise; but I do not believe he intends to be wise. The first reason is that up to now I have seen that whatever bad decisions the Emperor makes do not injure him, and all the good ones the King makes do not benefit him. It will be, as I have said, a bad plan for the Emperor to release the King; it will be a good one for the King to promise everything in order to be free. Nevertheless, because the King will keep it, the plan of the King will turn out bad and that of the Emperor good. The reasons that will make him observe it I have written to Filippo; they are these: he will have to leave his sons in prison; if he does not keep it, he will need to burden his kingdom, which is already burdened; he will need to burden the barons by sending them into Italy; he will have to turn at once to labors that, from past examples, are enough to

[1] Of France.

terrify him; and moreover he will be doing these things to aid the Church and the Venetians, who have helped to ruin him. And I wrote to you, and I write again, that great is the anger the King must feel against the Spaniards, but that cannot be much less than that which he must feel against the Italians.

I know well it can be said, and it would be true, that if through this hatred he lets Italy be ruined, he might then lose his kingdom. But the matter stands that he intends it thus, because, as soon as he is free, he will be in the midst of two difficulties, one, that of having Burgundy taken from him and losing Italy and being in the Emperor's power; and the second, in order to escape the first, to become almost a parricide and a breaker of faith. He would get into the above-mentioned difficulties in order to aid men who are disloyal and unstable, who for the slightest cause, after he had won, would make him lose again. So I lean to the opinion either that the King will not be free, or that, if he is free, he will keep his word; because dread of losing his kingdom, if Italy is lost (since he has, as you say, a French brain), is not going to move him in the way in which it might move some other man. The other opinion, that he will not believe Italy will go up in smoke, and perhaps will believe he can aid her, since she will have purged some of her sins, and he would have got his sons back and gained new strength. And if between them there were treaties for the division of spoil, so much the more the King would observe the treaties, but so much more the Emperor would be a crazy man to put back into Italy one whom he had got out of her; then he can chase out the Emperor himself.

I am telling you what I believe may be, but I do not at all say that for the King it would be the wiser decision, because he should imperil anew himself, his sons, and his kingdom in order to humble so hateful, feared, and dangerous a power. And the remedies for it seem to me these: to see that the King, as soon as he gets out, has near him one who, with his authority and his arguments and those of him who sends him, will make him forget past things and think of new ones, show him the unanimity of Italy, show him his plan as successful, if he decides to be that free king that he ought to wish to be. I believe that arguments and requests can have effect, but I believe that there would be much more effect in deeds.

I judge, in whatever way affairs go on, that there will be war, and soon, in Italy; therefore the Italians must see to it that they have France with them, and if they cannot have her, must consider how they are going to manage. I believe that in this situation we can make one of two decisions, either to be subject to the will of whoever comes, and to meet him with money and buy ourselves out; or truly to arm ourselves and with arms help ourselves as well as we can. I for my part do not expect that buying ourselves out and money will be enough, because if they would be enough, I should say, 'Let us stop here, and not consider further,' but they will not be enough, because either I am entirely blind or he will take from you first money and then life. If so, it will be a sort of vengeance on him for us to make sure that he will find us poor and used up, if we get nothing more from defending ourselves. Therefore I believe we should not defer arming ourselves, and should not wait for the decision of France, because the Emperor has leaders for his soldiers, has them in their places, can start war on his own terms when he pleases. It is necessary for us to prepare a force, whether hidden or open; otherwise we shall wake up one morning all bewildered. I should advise assembling forces secretly.

I say one thing that will seem crazy to you; I shall bring forward a plan that will seem to you either foolhardy or ridiculous; nonetheless these times demand decisions that

ld, unusual, and strange. You know, and everybody
s it who can think about this world, that the people
ncertain and foolish; nevertheless, even though they
ften they say that something is being done that should
be done. A few days ago it was said throughout Florence
that the Lord Giovanni de'Medici was raising the flag of
a soldier of fortune,[2] to make war where he had the best
opportunity. This rumor stirred up my spirit to imagine
that the people knew what ought to be done. I believe anyone who believes that among the Italians there
is no leader whom the soldiers would more gladly follow,[3]
and whom the Spanish more fear and more respect; everybody also thinks that Lord Giovanni is bold, prompt, has
great ideas, is a maker of great plans. We could then,
secretly making him strong, have him raise this flag, putting
under him as many cavalry and as many infantry as we can.
The Spanish would think this done craftily, and perhaps
would suspect both the King and the Pope, since Giovanni
is retained by the King; and if this happened, it would soon
make the brains of the Spanish spin around and they would
change their plans, though perhaps they have counted on
ruining Tuscany and the Church without any hindrance.
It could make the King change his opinions, and turn him
toward abandoning the treaty and choosing war, since he
would see that he has to do with people who are alive and,
in addition to arguments, show him deeds. And if we cannot use this method, and yet are to make war, I don't know
what we can do, and nothing else occurs to me; and tie
a string around your finger for this: if the King is not moved
by force and authority, and by things that are being done,

[2] Giovanni de'Medici, known to history as Giovanni of the Black Bands,
was the great-great-grandson of Giovanni, father of Cosimo, *Pater
Patriae*, as was Pope Clement VII. His mother was Catarina Sforza, the
Duchess of Forlì mentioned in *Prince* 20. Machiavelli gives in this letter
the general opinion of his military qualities. Mortally wounded in battle
against the Emperor's forces, he died 30 November 1526.

[3] Cf. *Prince*, chap. 26.

he will keep the treaty and leave you in the lurch, because, after he has come to Italy many times and you have either acted against him or stood looking on, he will not intend that this time also the same thing will happen to him.

The Barbera is there. If you can help her, I ask your interest, because I think much more of her than I do of the Emperor.

Niccolò Machiavelli.

No. 206

4 April 1526, Florence
To Francesco Guicciardini

[Before writing this letter, Machiavelli, when in Rome, had discussed the fortifications of Florence with Pope Clement VII. He is already looking forward, as it were, to his appointment, on 18 May or soon after, as secretary to the Procurators of the Walls. In this position he was in active charge of modernizing the mediaeval walls of the city.]

[The walls of Florence]

Your Magnificence My Honored Superior:

I received today about four o'clock yours of the first of the present month, and in the absence of Ruberto Acciaioli, who has gone to Monte Gufoni, I went at once to the Cardinal [1] and told him the intention of Our Ruler about the matters dealt with by Pietro Navarra,[2] and that His Holiness wished him to make so great and splendid a plan

[1] Cardinal Passerini, representing Pope Clement VII in Florence.

[2] Pietro Navarra, Count of Alvito, a Spanish veteran. When Ferdinand King of Spain refused to ransom him after he was taken prisoner at the battle of Ravenna in 1512, he entered the French service and later that of the allies against the Emperor Charles V. His expert opinion on the walls of Florence was desired by Pope Clement VII.

that it would give heart to a people like this one, and that they could hope to defend themselves against any serious and vigorous attack. His Most Reverend Lord said that he would have him come to him again this evening, and would make the request and charge him, in the most effective way he could, to produce such a thing. Nevertheless, having talked together of the plans presented, we conclude that, wishing to retain the old circuit, we can do no better, and that it is impossible not to retain that circuit; because deciding not to retain it, we must either increase Florence in the way known to His Holiness Our Lord, or take away the quarter of Santo Spirito and cut the city down to the level part only. The first method is made weak by the great garrison you would need, for which the people of Cairo would be too few.[3] The second method is partly weak and partly impious. It would be weak if you left the houses of that quarter standing, because you would leave a city to an enemy more powerful than you are, and who could make use of the country more than you could, so that he would vex you instead of your vexing him. As to the other way of destroying the quarter, everybody knows how difficult and unusual that would be. Therefore we must fortify the quarter as it stands. The method of doing so I do not wish to write to you as yet, both because it is not actually settled, and in order not to go ahead of my superiors. Let this be enough, that of the walls of the said quarter on the other side of Arno, part should be cut off, part advanced, part drawn back. I believe, and Signor Vitelli who has come for this purpose believes, that this city would then be very strong, stronger than the level portion. And so says and declares Count Pietro, declaring with oaths that this city, prepared in such a way, would become the strongest place in Italy. We are going to meet

[3] For the huge size of Cairo, see Ariosto, *Orlando Furioso* 15.63. Machiavelli read the poem in 1517 (Letter no. 166).

tomorrow morning to go over it all, and especially the larger plan. Then those who are assigned will meet and consider what has been ordered, and all will be put in writing and in a drawing, and will be sent to Rome to His Holiness Our Lord, and my opinion is that it will satisfy him, and especially that of the hill, where the unusual provisions are made. That of the plain does not depart from the ordinary, but because everybody knows how to make such sites strong, it matters little. Count Pietro will be here tomorrow and the next day, and we shall endeavor to get out of his head anything else that is there, and I have delayed in order to hear, so that it will not happen to me as to that Greek with Hannibal.[4] I thank you, etc.

Niccolò Machiavelli.

No. 207

17 May 1526, Florence
To Francesco Guicciardini

[See the head-note of the preceding letter.]

[The Pope's delays; the walls of Florence]

Magnificent Mr. President:

I have not written to you since I left there, because my head is so full of bastions that nothing else can come into it. The law is managed ordinarily in the way and with the method that in Rome is directed by His Holiness Our Lord. There is a delay in publishing the magistracy and in going ahead with the affair, until there comes from Rome a substitute for Chimenti Sciarpelloni, who they

---

[4] An inexperienced Greek talked on military matters in Hannibal's presence (Cicero, *De Oratore* 2.18).

say is in such bad health that he cannot attend to such things. It will be necessary also to have a supply for Antonio da Filicaia, who day before yesterday had an attack of apoplexy, and is in bad condition. It is strange that the Cardinal has not had a reply about Chimenti, and we fear some impediment; yet that is unlikely, since the matter is so far advanced.

I have heard the rumors from Lombardy, and it is recognized on every side how easy it would be to get some rascals from that region. This opportunity, for the love of God, should not be lost, and remember that Fortune, our bad advice, and worse officials would have brought not merely the King but the Pope to prison; he has been taken out by the bad advice of others and the same Fortune. Provide now, for the love of God, in such a way that His Holiness will not go back into the same dangers, from which you will never be secure until the Spanish are so completely driven out of Lombardy that they cannot return. I have a notion that the Emperor, seeing the King fail him, will make great offers to the Pope, which ought to find your ears stopped, if you recall the bad support and the threats that in the past have been made to you, and remember that the Duke of Sessa was accustomed to say that the Pope too late began to fear Caesar. Now God has brought things back to such a state that the Pope is in time to hold him, if this time is not lost. You know how many opportunities have been lost; do not lose this one or trust any more in standing still, turning yourself over to Fortune and to Time, because with Time there do not come always the same things, and Fortune is not always the same. I would say more, if I were talking to a man who did not know secrets and did not understand the world. Free Italy from long anxiety; root out these frightful beasts, which beyond the appearance and the voice have nothing human.

Here it is thought, if the fortifications go ahead, that I am to have the position of overseer and of secretary, and I am to be aided by one of my sons, and Daniello de' Ricci is to handle the money and all the records.

Niccolò Machiavelli.

No. 209

2 June 1526 (first letter), Florence
To Francesco Guicciardini

[See the head-note for Letter no. 206.]

[The Pope favors including more land within the walls of Florence]

Magnificent Mr. President:

I have not written to you for many days about the wall; now I shall tell you what comes to mind about it. Here it seems that the Pope has returned to the notion of the mountains, moved by the opinion of Giovanni del Bene, who in his letter says that in including all those hills there is more strength and less expense. As to strength, no city very large is ever strong, because its largeness confuses those who guard it, and many troubles can appear— which in those of convenient size does not happen. As to less expense, that is chatter, because he makes many assumptions that are not true. First, he says that all those mountains can be cut into for the space extending from the house of Bonciano to that of Matteo Bartoli outside the walls (which is, according to him, nineteen hundred feet, but is really over three thousand), so it is merely necessary to wall all the others. He says the cuts can be brought into use as a wall, and above them can be built a bank eight feet high and sixteen thick. This is not true, because there are countless places where because it is level there can be no cutting; further, all that cutting would not stand by itself and would wash down, so that it would have to be held up with a wall; then the banks around would cost a world, and would be disgraceful to this city, and in a very few years would have to be redone; so that the expense would be great and continuous, and bring little honor. He says that the city treasury could avail itself of eighty thousand ducats in value added to property, which is a fable, and he does not know what he is talking about, nor from where this added value could be got; so that to it seems improbable to everybody. Nonetheless we shall make the model the Pope has asked for and send it to him.

Until some special appropriation is made for this undertaking, it is necessary to spend the money that is here, and therefore the law lays down that the treasurer of the Signors should pay what money is now in the hands of the city, on whatever account any of it, both by the Signors and the officials, has been deposited with him. Nevertheless, Francesco del Nero will make trouble about paying, if His Holiness Our Lord does not write to him to pay it. The office has written about it to the ambassador. I beg you to aid in the matter, so that the Pope will write to him.

2 June 1526.

Niccolò Machiavelli.

No. 210

2 June 1526 (second letter), Florence
To Francesco Guicciardini

[See the head-note of Letter no. 206.]

[San Miniato as a fortress dangerous to Florentine liberty]

Though I know that your Luigi has written to you his opinion about putting the hill of San Miniato inside the wall, I too do not intend to omit writing you a word about it, because I think the matter very important.

The most harmful thing a republic can undertake is to erect something strong, or that easily can be made strong within its body. If you put before you the model that was left there, you will see that, when San Miniato is taken in and that bastion made up there, a fortress is created; because from the San Miniato Gate to that of San Niccolò the distance is so short that a hundred men in one day, by digging a ditch, could make it into a strong fortress. Then if ever through any misfortune a powerful man should come to Florence, as the King of France did in 1494,[1] you would become slaves without any protection,[2] because, since he would find the place open, you could not keep him from going in there, and since he could close it easily, you could not keep him from closing it. Consider it well and with what skill you can forestall it, and suggest the cutting-off, which is strong and not dangerous, because once the taking-in of San Miniato is begun, I fear the cutting-off would be too displeasing.

I have written these three letters separately, so that you can use each of them as is convenient.

Niccolò Machiavelli.

[1] Louis XII entered Florence as a conquered city.
[2] If a tyrant held the fortress of San Miniato he could control the city. For such a possibility see *Prince,* chap. 20.

No. 211

2 June 1526 (third letter), Florence
To Francesco Guicciardini

[See Letters nos 196, 199, 200.]

[The marriage negotiations once more]

Until last Saturday I did not have a chance to speak
with L[orenzo] S[trozzi], but being with him and discussing a number of things, he touched on his son, so I had
an opportunity to complain of his paying little attention to
the matter that I earlier brought before him, and said I
was certain that as once a rich marriage escaped him, now
one very honorable and not poor was going to escape him;
and I did not know, if he intended to give his son a
Florentine girl, where else he could go. He freely confessed
that I was telling the truth and that you had approached
him, and nothing could please him more; it pleased him
so much that even if the thing could not be done now, he
could suppose, since you have four, that he would be in
time for one. His reasons for putting it off are that his
wife's health is improved, and the boy has changed his
ways for the better, associating with educated men and
studying hard; he had thoughts of marrying him because
earlier he did neither of these two things. The third reason
is his daughter, whom he wishes to marry off first. But
the idea nevertheless pleases him so much that he already
has talked many times with the boy about you. When he
returned from Loreto, he took the opportunity of being
in Romagna two days with your Jacopo, who showed the
greatness of your position, and with what dignity you hold

it, and the name you have, and exalted your capacities to the sky. All this worked to make the thing easy when it was to be discussed, because he feared his son would get the notion of a big dower. Altogether he spoke on the affair in such a way that I could not wish more. I did not fail to show him that his hesitation is baseless, because the girl is of such an age that she can be kept unmarried four or five years, and that this match would aid him in marrying his daughter, because he who wants unusual dowers has to give them. I labored with him a bit, so if he were not a man a little set in his ways, I should have great hope in the matter.

Niccolò Machiavelli.

No. 219

5 November 1526, Florence
To Francesco Guicciardini

[See the head-note to Letter no. 202.]

[Machiavelli in Modena. Political ineptitude]

Mr Deputy:

From Modena[1] I wrote Your Lordship a letter more fitted to amuse Filicciago than to do anything else;[2] so I write what happened next.

So beginning at Modena, when I arrived Filippo [de' Nerli] met me and said: "Can it be that I have never done a thing that is right?" I replied with a laugh: "Mr

---

[1] In a letter of 30 October Guicciardini acknowledged Machiavelli's letter from Modena, which apparently is not now extant. In Alvisi's text a misprint makes Guicciardini Deputy of Modena and hides the place where Machiavelli wrote.

[2] Mentioned by Guicciardini in a letter of 12 November 1526.

Governor, don't be astonished at that, you are not at fault, but this year is, because not a person has done one thing well, nor is anything as it should be. The Emperor could not have conducted himself worse, not having for so long a time sent his men any aid, though he could easily have done so; the Spanish could now and then have played some big tricks on us, and have not known how; we could have won the war and have not known how; the Pope has trusted more in one penful of ink than in a thousand infantrymen, who would have been enough to guard him; the Sienese alone have conducted themselves well. It is no marvel if in a crazy time the crazy come out well.[3] So, my Lord Governor, it would be a worse sign to have carried through some good action than to have done a bad one." "Since that's the state of things," said Filippo, "I'm going to stop worrying and be quite happy." And so ended the first act of the comedy. Soon after came Count Guido, and when he saw me, he said: "Is the Deputy still angry?" I answered that he was not, because he no longer had near him the one who was the reason for his anger. And not to tell all the details, we talked a little of this blessed wrath of yours; and he said he would sooner go into exile in Egypt than serve in an army where you were. On that I said what was proper, and especially debated the bad and the good that your presence had brought about, so that easily everybody granted that it had done more good than harm. I remained in Modena two days, and conversed with a prophet who said, bringing up witnesses, that he had foretold the flight of the Pope and the uselessness of the enterprise, and again he says that not yet are we through with all the bad times, in which the Pope and we will suffer a great deal.

We came finally to Florence, and the greatest blame that I have heard given to you is that in letters written

[3] For an instance of Sienese madness, see The [Golden] Ass 1.23.

here to the Cardinal, you have shown the ease of the undertaking and its certain victory, whereupon I have said that
this is not possible, because I believe I have seen all the
important letters Your Lordship has written, in which there
were opinions entirely against certain victory.

Niccolò Machiavelli.

No. 219 B

November 1526,[1] Florence (?)
To Bartolomeo Cavalcanti

[See the head-note of Letter no. 202.]

[The military mistakes of Pope Clement VII]

Dearest Bartolomeo:

The reason why the Pope started this war before the
King of France sent his soldiers into Italy and took action
in Spain according to his agreement, and before all the
Swiss arrived, was his hope in the people of Milan, and
his belief that six thousand Swiss, whom the Venetians and
the Pope had sent on learning of the first rebellions in
Milan, would be so prompt that they would arrive at the
same time as the Venetians arrived with their army. Besides, he believed that the King's soldiers, if they were not
so prompt, would at least be early enough to aid in carrying
through the undertaking. To these hopes was joined the
needs of the Castle,[2] which was showing that it required

---

[1] The reference to All Saints' Day near the end of the letter puts its
date after October 31, 1526. The Spanish fleet, mentioned just before as
not yet arrived, reached Naples on December 1. This letter, not in Alvisi's
edition, is given by Tommaseo, *Vita di Machiavelli* 2.1251.
[2] Of Milan.

aid. All these things, then, made the Pope hasten, and with such hope that we believed this war would end in fifteen days; this hope was increased by the capture of Lodi. The armies of the Venetians and of the Pope did unite, then; but of the presuppositions above, two of the most important were lacking, because the Swiss did not come, and the people of Milan were of no value. Hence, when we appeared before Milan, the people did not stir, and not having the Swiss, we did not have courage to stay there, and retired to Marignano, and did not return to Milan until five thousand Swiss had come. Their coming, as earlier it would have been useful, was harmful, because it gave us courage to return to Milan in order to relieve the Castle, and it was not relieved, and we committed ourselves to remaining there, because, the first retirement having been shameful, nobody advised the second.

This caused the attempt on Cremona to be made with part of the infantry and not with all, as it would have been made if on the loss of the Castle we had been at Marignano. For these reasons, then, and also since we expected it to be easy, we carried on the affair of Cremona weakly. This was contrary to a rule of mine that says it is not a wise plan to risk all one's fortune but not all one's forces. They believed, because of the fortress, that four thousand soldiers would be enough to capture her. This attack, because it was weak, made Cremona more difficult, because those forces did not assail, but did point out, the weak places; as a result those inside did not lose them but strengthened them. Furthermore, they settled their courage to the defense; hence, although later the Duke of Urbino went there, and there were fourteen thousand soldiers round about, they were not enough; while if he had been there early with the whole army—able at one time to make several attacks—of necessity they would have taken her in six days, and perhaps this campaign would have been won, because we would have had the prestige of the capture, along with a very large army. Because, since thirteen thousand Swiss came, either Milan or Genoa, or perhaps both of them, would have been mastered. And the enemy would have had no recourse; the troubles at Rome would not have occurred; the reinforcements, which have not yet come, would not have been in time. And we have spent fifty days hoping for Milan, and the capture of Cremona is brought about late, when all our affairs have gone to ruin.

We have then on our side lost this war twice; once when we went to Milan and did not stay there; the second time when we sent and did not go to Cremona. The reason for the first was the timidity of the Duke; of the second, the vanity of us all, because, feeling disgraced by the first retreat, nobody dared advise the second. The Duke could do badly against the will of all; against the will of all he could not do well. These are the errors that have taken victory away from us; I say *taken it away* through our not having conquered early; because we might have deferred but not lost the campaign, if our bad arrangements had not been added. These also have been two; the first is that the Pope has not raised money in times when he could with reputation have done so, and in the ways used by other popes. The other is that he remained in Rome in such a condition that he could be captured like a baby—something that has snarled this skein up in such a way that Christ could not straighten it out, because the Pope has taken his soldiers from the field, and Messer Francesco is still in the field, and today the Duke of Urbino must have arrived there. Many leaders, of many opinions, are left, but all ambitious and unbearable, and, lacking anybody who knows how to assuage their factions and keep them united, they will be a chorus of dogs.[3] From this results a confusion in our doings that is very great, and already Lord Giovanni

[3] Cf. the quarrelsome leaders of *Prince* 26.

does not intend to remain there, and I believe that today he will leave. These bad arrangements were all corrected by the eagerness and effort of Messer Francesco. Besides this, if money has been coming sparingly from Rome, now it will fail entirely. So I see little order in our houses, and if God does not aid us to the south, as he has done to the north, we have few resources left.

Because, as, with the ruin of Hungary, he impeded aid from Germany for the northerners, so he will need to impede aid from Spain with the ruin of the fleet; hence we need to have Juno go to beseech Aeolus for us and promise him *la Contessa* and all the ladies in Florence,[4] so that he will give full freedom to the winds in our favor. And without doubt, if it were not for the Turk, I believe the Spanish would have come to celebrate All Saints' Day with us.

I, having seen the Castle lost, and observed how the Spaniards have established themselves in three or four of those cities and made themselves sure of the people, judged that this war was going to be long, and through its length dangerous. Because I know with what difficulty cities are taken when there is somebody inside who means to defend them, and that a province is taken in a day, but a city requires months and years to take, as is shown by many ancient narratives, and in modern times by Rhodes and Hungary. For that reason I wrote to Francesco Vettori that I believed we could not support this undertaking, except to bring about that the King of France should take Milan (we should give him that state), or possibly as a diversion through which we would leave the frontiers of these states guarded, so that the Spanish could not make progress. The Pope then with all his forces should attack the Kingdom, which I believe could be taken before one of these cities here. Because there would be neither obstinate

Aeneid 1.65ff.

defenders nor peoples conquered [5] . . . , such as a man
would like. Besides this, the war would feed itself,[6] because
in addition to the assistance he could have from the cities,
he would have tribute, and the richness of the country, not
ravaged, would make assistance more lasting. Also the
Pope without new expense would live securely in Rome,
and we would see which the Emperor estimated higher,
Lombardy or the Kingdom. And if this is not done, I look
on the war as lost, because its length is sure, and in length
dangers can be reckoned as certain, either through lack of
money or through other accidents such as those that have
come up. And it has seemed to me a strange plan to wear
ourselves out in the field, and that the enemy should be at
ease in the city, and that, when at last his reinforcements
came, finding us worn out, he should ruin us like the Ad-
miral and the King.

[Niccolò Machiavelli.]

No. 222

2 April 1527, Imola
To Guido Machiavelli, in Florence

[The study of letters and music;
a rural problem; the family]

My dearest son Guido:

I have received your letter, which has been a great
pleasure to me, especially since you write that you are completely cured, because I could not have better news. For

[5] Something is lacking from the manuscript.
[6] I have accepted Tommaseo's emendation of the ms reading (*contesa*).

if God grants life to you and to me, I believe I can make you a man of standing, if you wish to play your part as you should, because, beside' the great friendships I have, I have made a new friendship with the Cardinal Cibo (it is so great that I myself wonder at it) which will be of service to you. But it is necessary for you to learn and, since you no longer have the excuse of sickness, to work hard to learn letters and music, since you see how much I am aided by the little skill I have. So, my son, if you wish to give pleasure to me and bring prosperity and honor to yourself, do well and learn, because if you help yourself, everybody will help you.

The little mule, though he is crazy, needs to be treated quite differently from other crazy creatures; because the other crazy ones are tied up, and I want you to untie him. Give him to Vangelo and tell him to lead him onto Monte Pugliano and then take off his bridle and halter and let him go where he will to get his living and rid himself of his madness. The territory is large; the animal is small; he can't do any harm. And so without taking any trouble about it, we can see what he wants to do, and you will be in time, whenever he gets his wits back, to catch him again. With the horses do what Lodovico has told you to do; he, I thank God, has got well, and he has sold out. And I know that he has prospered, since he has sent money, but I wonder and feel bad because he has not written.

Greet Mona Marietta and tell her that I have been on the point of leaving here every day, and still I remain; and I never had so much desire to be in Florence as now; but I can do nothing else. Merely say to her that for anything I hear she can be sure that I shall be there before there is any trouble. Kiss Baccina, Piero, and Totto, if he is there, and I would have been glad to know whether his eyes are cured. Be happy and spend as little as you can. And remind Bernardo that he should try to do well; to whom within fifteen days I have written two letters and have had no reply. Christ watch over you all.

Niccolò Machiavelli, in Imola.

No. 223

5 April 1527, Forlì
To Francesco Vettori, in Florence

[See the head-note for Letter no. 202.]

[What policy for Pope Clement VII?]

My honored Francesco:

Since the truce was made at Rome, and we saw that the Emperor's soldiers there did not intend to keep it, Messer Francesco wrote to Rome that it was necessary to take one of three courses: either go back to war in such a way that all the world should understand that never more were we going to discuss peace, in order that France, the Venetians, and everybody, without hesitation or suspicion, should do his duty (in his letter he showed that there were also many possibilities, especially in an attempt to aid the Pope). Or if this did not suit, we should adopt the second, which would be wholly contrary to the first, namely, enter into this peace with complete effort, and put our heads in the lap of this vicar,[1] and in this way let ourselves be controlled by Fortune. Or indeed, if worn out in the first of these two courses, and disgraced by the second, we might take a third course, which does not matter and need not be mentioned now. Today Messer Francesco has received a reply from Rome, that the Pope has turned to take this

(handwritten margin note: Sack of Rome)

---

[1] Lannoy, the viceroy of Naples.

245

second course of throwing himself wholly into the lap of the vicar and of peace, which if it succeeds will be now our safety; if it does not succeed, it will cause us to be wholly abandoned by everybody. If it is going to succeed or not, you can judge as well as we can; but I say to you only this, that Messer Francesco has taken in any event this decision, to aid in the affairs of Romagna, while he sees that at sixteen soldi to the lira they can be defended, but when he sees them indefensible, without any hesitation he will abandon them; and with those Italian forces he can find, and with such money as is left to him, will come in this direction to save Florence and her state in any way he can. And be in good hope, for it will be defended no matter what.

This imperial army is strong and large; nevertheless, if it did not encounter those who abandoned themselves, it would not capture a bake-oven. But there is danger that through weakness one town at the beginning will yield to it, and when one does so, all the others go up in smoke; this is one of the things that make the defense of this province risky. Nonetheless, if it is lost, you, if you do not abandon yourselves, can save yourselves; and by defending Pisa, Pistoia, Prato, and Florence, you will get an agreement with them that, if it is heavy, will not at the end be mortal. And because that decision by the Pope is still secret with respect to these allies, and for every other respect, I pray you not to make this letter public. Farewell.

Niccolò Machiavelli, in Forlì.

14 April 1527, Forlì
To Francesco Vettori, in Florence

[See the head-note of Letter no. 202.]

[An unsatisfactory peace]

Magnificent Sir:

The agreement has always been advised here for the same reasons for which you there have always advised it; because, having seen the conduct of France and of the Venetians, having seen the poor discipline of our soldiers, having seen that the Pope lacked all hope of being able to keep up the war in the Kingdom, having seen the power and obstinacy of the enemy, we judged the war lost, as you yourself, when I left there, judged it. This has led us always to advise agreement, but we meant an agreement which would be solid, and not uncertain and confused like this, which is made in Rome and not kept in Lombardy, and that there should be a little money here. That little we would need to keep to use in such an uncertain agreement, and we would continue unarmed; or in order to arm ourselves, we would spend the money, and be left without any for the agreement. And so, whereas we thought that a clear agreement would bring safety, a confused one is wholly pernicious and our ruin.

From there it is now written that the agreement is almost settled, and because the first pay is 60 thousand scudi, we rely for the greater part on the money that is here. Here we have 13 thousand ducats in cash and seven to our credit with the Venetians. If the enemy begin to attack Tuscany, it will be necessary to spend them in maintaining these soldiers, in order to try to hold this poor city, so that if you rely on the agreement, you will have to rely on an agreement that will end these armies and these expenses. Otherwise, if we keep up a confused agreement that requires us to provide for both the agreement and the war, we shall not provide for either of them, and the result will be evil for us and good for our enemies, who, marching toward us, are giving their attention to war, and letting you confuse yourselves between war and agreements. I am yours.

Your Niccolò Machiavelli, in Forlì.

No. 225

16 April 1527, Forlì
To Francesco Vettori, in Florence

[See the head-note of Letter no. 202.]

[I love my native city more than my soul]

Magnificent, etc.:

Monseigneur de La Motte has been today in the camp of the imperials with the final form of the agreement made there, and if Bourbon accepts, he must halt his army. If he moves, it is a sign that he does not wish any agreement; so tomorrow will be the judge of our affairs. Therefore it is decided here, if tomorrow he moves, to think on war completely, without having a hair that thinks further of peace; if he does not move, to think of peace, and to lay aside all thought of war. With this north wind we too have to sail and, deciding on war, to cut off all the affairs of peace, and in such a way that the allies will come on without any hesitation, because now we cannot hobble any more but must go like mad; and often desperation finds remedies that choice cannot find.

They are coming without artillery, into a difficult region. Hence if we, with what little life remains to us, unite with the forces of the League that are ready, either they will leave this province with shame or they will come down to reasonable terms.

I love Messer Francesco Guicciardini; I love my native city more than my own soul; and I tell you this through that experience given me by sixty years, namely, that I do not believe that ever more difficult articles than these were struggled with, where peace is necessary and war cannot be abandoned; and to have on our hands a prince who scarcely is able to deal with peace alone or with war alone.

I send you my regards.

Niccolò Machiavelli, in Forlì.

No. 227

18 April 1527, Brisighella
To Francesco Vettori, in Florence

[See the head-note for Letter no. 202.]

[Those who gain from war will not praise peace]

Honored Francesco:

These French soldiers have been miraculously brought here to Brisighella; and likewise it will be a miracle if the Duke of Urbino comes to Pianoro tomorrow (as it seems that the Legate of Bologna writes from there); and here we shall wait, as I believe, to learn what he does. And for the love of God, if you cannot obtain this agreement, cut off the negotiation right now, and in such a way, with letters and with actions, that these allies will aid us; because as the agreement, if it were observed, would be in every way the certainty of our safety, so to negotiate about it without carrying it through will be the certainty of our ruin. And that the agreement was necessary will be seen if it is not made; and if Count Guido says something else, he is a fool. And only this I wish to argue with him: You ask him if it is possible to keep them from coming into Tuscany, and he will say it is not, if he says what he has always said in the past; and similarly the Duke of Urbino. If it is true that they cannot be kept out, ask him how they can be got out without fighting a battle, and how fit this city is to endure two armies in her territory, when the friendly army is more unbearable than the hostile one. If he settles this for you, tell him he is right. But they who profit from war, as these soldiers do, would be fools if they praised peace. But God will give them more war than we shall like.

Niccolò Machiavelli, in Brisighella.

List of Familiar Letters in This Edition

Number (Alvisi)	Written to	Date
3	Ricciardo Bechi	9 March 1498
103	Luigi Guicciardini	20 November 1509
115	An unidentified lady	September 1512
116	Piero Soderini	January 1513
117	Francesco Vettori	15 March 1513
119	" "	18 March 1513
120	" "	9 April 1513
122	" "	16 April 1513
128	" "	29 April 1513
124	" "	20 June 1513
125	Giovanni Vernacci	26 June 1513
129	" "	4 August 1513
131	Francesco Vettori	10 August 1513
133	" "	25 August 1513
134	" "	26 August 1513
135	" "	August 1513
137	" "	10 December 1513
138	" "	19 December 1513
140	" "	5 January 1514
142	" "	4 February 1514
144	" "	25 February 1514
145	" "	16 April 1514
146	Giovanni Vernacci	20 April 1514
148	Francesco Vettori	10 June 1514
150	" "	3 August 1514
152	" "	4 December 1514
154	" "	20 December 1514
155	" "	" " "

Number (Alvisi)	Written to	Date
156	" "	" " "
159	" "	31 January 1515
160	Giovanni Vernacci	18 August 1515
161	" "	19 November 1515
162	" "	15 February 1516
163	Paolo Vettori	10 October 1516
164	Giovanni Vernacci	8 June 1517
166	Lodovico Alamanni	17 December 1517
167	Giovanni Vernacci	5 January 1518
168	" "	25 January 1518
169	" "	16 April 1520
175	Francesco del Nero	8 November 1520
179	Francesco Guicciardini	17 May 1521
182	" "	18 May 1521
183	" "	19 May 1521
185	Francesco del Nero	26 September 1523
186	Francesco Guicciardini	30 August 1524
192	" "	3 August 1525
196	" "	17 August 1525
198	" "	September 1525
199	" "	November (?) 1525
200	" "	19 December 1525
202	" "	3 January 1526
204	" "	15 March 1526
206	" "	4 April 1526
207	" "	17 May 1526
209	" "	2 June 1526
210	" "	" " "
211	" "	" " "
219	" "	5 November 1526
219B	Bartolomeo Cavalcanti	November 1526
222	Guido Machiavelli	2 April 1527
223	Francesco Vettori	5 April 1527
224	" "	14 April 1527
225	" "	16 April 1527
227	" "	18 April 1527